From Seven Rivers to Ten Thousand Lakes

From Seven Rivers to Ten Thousand Lakes

Minnesota's Indian American Community

Preeti Mathur

Foreword by Dr. S. K. Dash

MINNESOTA
HISTORICAL
SOCIETY PRESS

The publication of this book was supported through a generous grant from the Dr. Dash Foundation.

mnhspress.org

The Minnesota Historical Society Press is a member of the Association of University Presses.

Manufactured in the United States of America

10 9 8 7 6 5 4 3 2 1

∞ The paper used in this publication meets the minimum requirements of the American National Standard for Information Sciences—Permanence for Printed Library Materials, ANSI Z39.48-1984.

International Standard Book Number
ISBN: 978-1-68134-114-9 (paper)

Library of Congress Cataloging-in-Publication Data is available upon request.

Population chart, page 6: Cameron, Anjuli M. Analysis of US Census Bureau statistics, from 1910–2010 decennial census. Council on Asian Pacific Minnesotans.

Occupation chart, page 6: Chaudhuri, Sanjukta. Analysis of American Community Survey, 2011–15. Labor Market Information Office, Minnesota Department of Employment and Economic Development.

Demographic details, page 6: Minnesota State Demographic Center, Department of Administration. *The Economic Status of Minnesotans 2018.*

Sales chart, page 8: 2012 Survey of Business Owners. "Statistics for All U.S. Firms by Industry, Gender, Ethnicity, and Race for the U.S., States, Metro Areas, Counties, and Places: 2012." Open Data Soft.

Population chart, page 29: "Percentage of Indians (Asian) in Minnesota by City." Zip Atlas.

Cover images: front, top: Dixit family, 1962, *Nayana Ramakrishnan*; Ragamala Dance Company performance, *MNHS*; front, middle: Mitra patent, *MNHS*; Khazana Gallery, *MNHS*; Niru Misra, Pillsbury Elementary, *Niru Misra*; Hindu Mandir, *Morgan Sheff*; front, bottom: Ram Gada departs for USA, *Ram Gada*; IndiaFest, *MNHS*; back, top to bottom: Nirmala Rajasekar performance, *MNHS*; celebrating Rathayatra, *Hindu Mandir*; Indian Students Association, *University of Minnesota*; snowshoeing, *author*

Contents

Publisher's Note   vii

Foreword by Dr. S. K. Dash   ix

1 Introduction and Overview   3

2 Coming to Minnesota   11

3 Settling Down, Adapting, and Assimilating   29

4 Preserving Culture, Heritage, Family Values, and Traditions   35

5 Dealing with Discrimination, Adversity, and Loss   77

6 Spotlighting Segments of the Indian Population   83

7 Contributing to Minnesota   91

8 Looking into the Future   121

Acknowledgments   123

Sources Consulted   125

For Further Reading   126

Index   127

Publisher's Note

The Minnesota Historical Society is proud and honored to publish *From Seven Rivers to Ten Thousand Lakes: Minnesota's Indian American Community*. The contributions and achievements of Indian Americans are a vital part of this state's history and have enriched people and communities throughout Minnesota. Indian Americans have attained great levels of educational and professional success here, bringing innovation and culture to the benefit of all Minnesotans. Their impact has been felt in a range of industries, most notably the engineering, technology, computer, and medical fields. Indian cultural festivals are held throughout the year in the state, and the Hindu Temple of Minnesota in suburban Maple Grove is one of the largest Hindu temples in the United States, drawing people from throughout the upper Midwest for a variety of religious, cultural, and community services.

In *From Seven Rivers to Ten Thousand Lakes*, author and longtime Twin Cities Indian American resident Preeti Mathur chronicles the experiences and contributions of Indian Americans in Minnesota over the past century, including both the history of their arrival and the contemporary work being done in business, education, the arts, and more, helping to lead Minnesota into the new century. She has brought together stories from many generations of Indian Americans and presented them within the context of the challenges and opportunities encountered in their new home. This book demonstrates how Indian Americans in Minnesota, now more than forty thousand strong, have secured their place in the history, economy, and culture of our state.

The Minnesota Historical Society is indebted to Dr. S. K. Dash and the Dr. Dash Foundation for providing the financial support to allow us to publish this work. Dr. Dash has long been an influential figure in the community, and his philanthropy, leadership, and innovation have proven invaluable to building the Indian American community in Minnesota. From his pioneering work in the probiotics field to his charitable giving, Dr. Dash has been helping the Indian American community in Minnesota grow and prosper for nearly half a century.

Josh Leventhal
Director, MNHS Press

Foreword

The major contributions that Indian Americans have made to Minnesota's economy, culture, and history are remarkable given the relatively short duration of our presence in the state. Today, Indian Americans can be found in leadership positions in virtually every field.

In academia, we have Devinder Malhotra, the chancellor of Minnesota State University, and Sri Zaheer, the dean of the Carlson School of Management at the University of Minnesota.

In business, we have luminaries such as Mahendra Nath of Nath Companies, who was inducted into the Minnesota Business Hall of Fame in 2002. The next generations are full of innovative entrepreneurs who will keep Minnesota in the limelight, such as Deepinder Singh, founder and CEO of 75F. The technology revolution has brought many IT professionals from India to the United States and to Minnesota.

In the field of government, Neel Kashkari serves as president of the Federal Reserve Bank of Minneapolis. Gopal Khanna was Minnesota's first chief information officer, appointed by Governor Tim Pawlenty, and he serves in President Donald Trump's administration as director of the Agency for Healthcare Research and Quality.

In the arts, we have Dipankar Mukherjee, founder of Pangea World Theater, a community-centered, multidisciplinary theater based in Minneapolis; Ranee Ramaswamy, who founded the Ragamala Dance Company, which has been recognized by the National Endowment of the Arts; and Rita Mustaphi, the artistic director of Katha Dance Theatre, which has presented to audiences locally, nationally, and internationally, including at Carnegie Hall in New York City.

These names, and indeed those presented throughout this book, are only a representative sampling of Indian Americans who have contributed to and prospered in the state of Minnesota.

Yet, as we celebrate the achievements of the Indian American community, we also need to be cognizant of the checkered history of acceptance of our community in the United States.

President Trump's Muslim ban in January 2017 did not mark the first time that the United States targeted a particular group for exclusion. National security has been used as a rationale for excluding immigrants for decades. It began with the Chinese Exclusion Act of 1882 and was followed by attempts to pass a Hindu Exclusion bill. The problem was, ethnologists and linguists had suggested that Indians belonged to the same racial family (Caucasians) as Europeans. Nevertheless, the Supreme Court, in 1923, declared that "Hindus" were racially disqualified from citizenship.

Only with passage of the Immigration and Nationality Act of 1965 did the end come to these conspicuous forms of government-sanctioned racial and ethnic discrimination. Soon after, the first wave of recent immigrants from India began to arrive on these shores.

The quotas established by earlier immigration laws to restrict the number of immigrants that could come from each country disproportionately affected India because of its large population. One positive consequence, however, was that the early immigrants from India tended to be well-educated professionals, such as doctors and engineers, which helped to set in motion the label of Indians as the "model immigrant."

While most immigrants from India settled on the coasts, Minnesota has long been a destination for men and women seeking opportunities for education and in a wide range of professional fields, especially technology and health care. Indian Americans in Minnesota have inspiring stories to tell. These stories, of our friends and neighbors, are of everyday people who are helping the great state of Minnesota thrive and prosper. This book seeks to share those stories and to highlight the contributions of the state's vibrant Indian American community.

My sincere thanks to Preeti Mathur and the Minnesota Historical Society for making this publication possible.

Dr. S. K. Dash
Chairman and Founder, UAS Laboratories, LLC
President and Founder, DD Innovations, Inc.
Chairman and Founder, Dr. Dash Foundation

From Seven Rivers to Ten Thousand Lakes

79TH CONGRESS
1ST SESSION

S. 331

IN THE SENATE OF THE UNITED STATES

JANUARY 18, 1945

Mr. BALL introduced the following bill; which was read twice and referred to the Committee on Immigration

A BILL

To authorize the naturalization and the admission into the United States under a quota of Eastern Hemisphere Indians of India and descendants of Eastern Hemisphere Indians of India.

1   *Be it enacted by the Senate and House of Representa-*
2 *tives of the United States of America in Congress assembled,*
3 That so much of section 303 of the Nationality Act of 1940,
4 as amended, or precedes the proviso, is amended to read as
5 follows:
6   "SEC. 303. The right to become a naturalized citizen
7 under the provisions of this Act shall extend only to white
8 persons, persons of African nativity or descent, descendants

1 Introduction and Overview

Dr. Padmakar K. Dixit, his wife, and their two daughters in Minnesota, 1962. *Courtesy Nayana Ramakrishnan*

"I am going to America on a jet! I am going to fly in a Boeing 707!" Seven-year-old Nayana Dixit recalls shouting these words to anyone who would listen in her birth city of Pune, in Western India. It was the early 1960s, and after many frustrating visits to the US embassy in Mumbai (then called Bombay), her mother, older sister, and she were finally granted visas to travel to the United States to join her father, Dr. Padmakar K. Dixit. Dr. Dixit, a biochemist, had come to Minnesota in 1958 to run the anatomy lab at the University of Minnesota. In January 1961, about a week after John F. Kennedy's inauguration and two years after Dr. Dixit had arrived, the Dixits became one of the first Indian families to settle down in Minnesota.

Since those early days, Indian Americans in Minnesota, just like their counterparts in other regions of the United States, have established themselves as a vital and growing immigrant group.

Unlike other Asian immigrants, Indians did not come to Minnesota as refugees of war. The influx of Indians in Minnesota can be traced to three distinct waves around the milestone Immigration and Nationality Act of 1965. While Indians arrived in other parts of the country as farmers and railroad workers, most came to Minnesota for education. Later, many arrived to take jobs in Minnesota's technology companies (see "Coming to Minnesota," pages 11–28). Indian Americans have come to Minnesota not just from India but from other countries as well (see "Indian Diaspora," pages 23–28), settling largely in the Twin Cities suburbs (see "Settlement Patterns," pages 29–30).

Compared to other immigrants, Indians are better educated and higher earners, working largely as professionals—engineers, doctors, and professors. Many are creative entrepreneurs who run start-ups and thriving businesses (see "Quick Stats and Facts on Indian Americans," pages 5–9). Almost all speak English and assimilate well (see "Assimilating and Adapting," pages 30–33).

Like other Asians, Indians tend to be family centered; they also tend to preserve their culture, traditions, and ties to their heritage. Many consider religion an important aspect of life and regularly participate in their own faith groups and in places of worship that they have built (see "Preserving Culture, Heritage, Family Values, and Traditions," pages 35–75). Like other immigrants, they believe in the value of hard work and are determined to overcome adversities, obstacles, and discrimination (see "Dealing with Discrimination, Adversity, and Loss," pages 77–82).

Over the years, Indians have made significant contributions to Minnesota's landscape through their professions, businesses, and culture, as well as through their volunteerism and philanthropy (see "Contributing to Minnesota," pages 91–120).

> **Indians, Asian Indians, or Indian Americans?**
> Ever since Christopher Columbus mistakenly landed in America and referred to the natives as *Indians,* there has been confusion on how to refer to immigrants from India and its diaspora.
> In 1980, the US Census introduced the term *Asian Indian.* However, since this phrase does not include the word *American,* it was unacceptable to those who viewed themselves as Americans as well. Hence, the term *Indian Americans* is used in this book.

About this Book

This book attempts to chronicle more than sixty years of Indian Americans in Minnesota and to provide details on the community's broad characteristics. That said, generalizing about the Indian community is not an easy task. Few immigrant groups in the United States come from a country as diverse as India, with its many languages, religions, and social and cultural practices. Indians settling in Minnesota have brought this diversity with them. *From Seven Rivers to Ten Thousand Lakes* captures some of the diversity, but it is not intended to be an all-encompassing book on Indian history and culture or a who's who of Indians in Minnesota. Instead, it offers glimpses of various aspects of the Indian community with the hope that these serve as a springboard to real and meaningful discourses with Indian friends, colleagues, and neighbors. It is said, *Communication is the beginning of understanding.*

Another goal of this book is to document the history and experiences of the early Indian American settlers before these people and their stories are lost to time. While it is impossible to document everyone's experiences, we hope the stories and profiles in this book will encourage second- and third-generation Indians to interact with their elders and record their own family's stories. For those from the Indian community's pioneer days, we hope some of these stories and images bring smiles and resurrect additional memories and nostalgia to share with family and friends. For those Indians who have arrived more recently, we hope this book gives a historical perspective to reflect on and compare with their own experiences.

This book is meant to appeal to both casual readers and those seeking in-depth information on Indians in Minnesota. Although not an academic treatise, it draws on details gleaned from research in the Minnesota Historical Society's archives, including several oral histories, as well as from US census data and statistics. However, a good part of the narrative comes from the collective memories of community members as well as from the author's own "tribal knowledge" gained from living in the community for more than forty years. In short, this book has something for everyone.

Note: Since most Indians reside in the Twin Cities, much of the information shared here pertains to those living in this area.

QUICK STATS AND FACTS ON INDIAN AMERICANS

Population: Since 1980, when the census bureau began counting Indian Americans (as "Asian Indians"), the population of Indians in Minnesota has grown steadily, doubling every ten years. In 1980, only 3,670 Indian Americans lived in Minnesota. By 1990, their numbers had grown to 6,671 (0.2 percent of Minnesota's population) and by 2017 to 43,379 (0.8 percent of Minnesota's population). Minnesota has the seventeenth-largest Indian American population in the country; California and New York are ranked first and second, respectively. Most of Minnesota's Indian American population is young, with the median age being thirty years.

Asian Indians came to Minnesota from various regions in the world, about 90 percent from Asia, generally India, and others from Latin America, Africa, and Europe. More than 80 percent of them have a college education—bachelor's degree and beyond—and more than 96 percent speak English fluently. Fifty-six percent of the Indian population has been in Minnesota for fewer than ten years, and most who arrived recently listed computer-related occupations. More than 82 percent of the population in 2017 lived in households of more than one person; 18 percent were single.

Those who arrived before 1990 took up occupations in engineering (16 percent), academia (14 percent, mostly university professors), health care (5 percent),

> **Immigration Laws that Have Affected Indians**
>
> Discriminatory US immigration laws prevented Asians, including Indians, from immigrating to the United States. These laws included the Immigration Act of 1917 (also known as the Asiatic Barred Zone Act) and the National Origins Act (1924), which established a quota system heavily favoring people from northern and western Europe. However, in 1946, the Luce-Celler Act, signed by President Harry Truman, lifted some of these restrictions, allowing a quota of one hundred Indians to immigrate. It also allowed Indians already living in the United States (about 2,500–3,000) to become naturalized American citizens.
>
> When the Civil Rights Act of 1964 passed, it brought attention to race issues and encouraged major immigration reform. A year later, President Lyndon Johnson passed the Immigration and Nationality Act of 1965, which ended years of immigration restrictions based on race and national origins and opened the doors to many people of the world, including those from India. This act also made provisions for issuing visas based on family reunification.
>
> When the Immigration Act of 1990 created the H-1B visa to allow US employers to hire skilled foreign workers and professionals, hundreds of Indians arrived in Minnesota as "priority workers."

Asian Indian Population in Minnesota

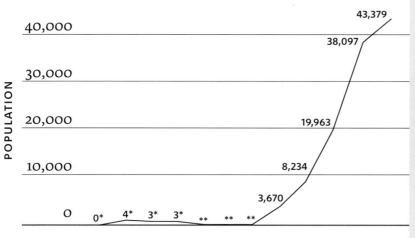

POPULATION

40,000 — 43,379

38,097

30,000

20,000 — 19,963

10,000 — 8,234

3,670

O   0*   4*   3*   3*   **   **   **

1910 1920 1930 1940 1950 1960 1970 1980 1990 2000 2010 2017

CENSUS YEARS

*Identified as "Hindu" by US Census
**Between 1950 and 1970, Asian Indian counts were not included as an individual race category. For the 1950 and 1960 US Census, Asian Indians were included in the "Other Race" category. For the 1970 US Census, Asian Indians were included in the "White" category.

Occupations of Indian Americans in Minnesota, 1990 and 2017

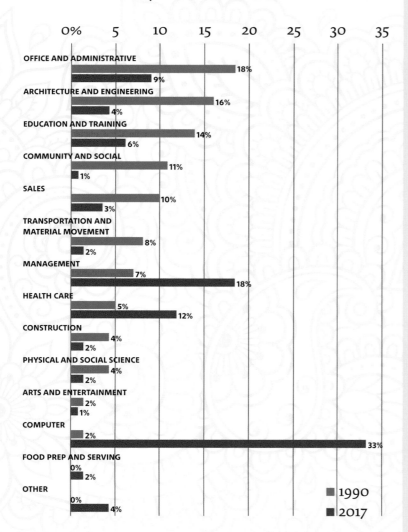

| | 0% | 5 | 10 | 15 | 20 | 25 | 30 | 35 |

OFFICE AND ADMINISTRATIVE — 18% / 9%
ARCHITECTURE AND ENGINEERING — 16% / 4%
EDUCATION AND TRAINING — 14% / 6%
COMMUNITY AND SOCIAL — 11% / 1%
SALES — 10% / 3%
TRANSPORTATION AND MATERIAL MOVEMENT — 8% / 2%
MANAGEMENT — 7% / 18%
HEALTH CARE — 5% / 12%
CONSTRUCTION — 4% / 2%
PHYSICAL AND SOCIAL SCIENCE — 4% / 2%
ARTS AND ENTERTAINMENT — 2% / 1%
COMPUTER — 2% / 33%
FOOD PREP AND SERVING — 0% / 2%
OTHER — 0% / 4%

■ 1990
■ 2017

Demographics of Indian Americans in Minnesota

GEOGRAPHIC MOBILITY

0–10 years 54%

11+ years 46%

ENGLISH FLUENCY *abcd*

4% ⇒ Not fluent

96% ⇒ Fluent

HOUSEHOLD SIZE

🚶 1 person 18% 🚶

🚶🚶 2–3 people 55% 🚶🚶

🚶🚶🚶 4+ people 27% 🚶🚶🚶

🚶🚶🚶🚶 with children 49% 🚶🚶🚶🚶

EDUCATIONAL ATTAINMENT 🎓

85% → BACHELOR'S DEGREE OR HIGHER

44% → ADVANCED DEGREE

BIRTHPLACE

76% ❤ foreign born

18% ❤ Minnesota born

6% ❤ born in other US state or territory

YEARS IN UNITED STATES

0–10 ❤ 54%

11+ ❤ 46%

INDIVIDUALS AGES 16–64 IN THE LABOR FORCE

78% | participating

19% | not participating

3% | unemployed

management (7 percent), and computers (2 percent). In 2017, a large percentage (66 percent) of Asian Indians were either in computers (33 percent) or professions like engineering, medicine, or management (33 percent).

Just prior to and after 2000 (Y2K), the focus shifted from engineering to computers, with a larger portion of Indian Americans in Minnesota moving into management ranks in the corporations where they worked. Between 1990 and 2017, the occupation categories grew from 2 to 33 percent in computers, 7 to 18 percent in management, and 5 to 12 percent in health care—overall a 59 percent increase in the areas of computers (software) and management (as directors, vice presidents, and chief executive officers at Fortune 500 companies and founders of technology businesses). Engineering decreased from 16 to 4 percent and education decreased from 14 to 6 percent.

Among Minnesota's foreign-born, working-age population, Indians and Ethiopians are the groups with the greatest share of newer arrivals (within the past ten years).

:: Indians are highly mobile, reflecting the community's large share of new international arrivals.
:: Ninety-six percent of Indian Americans speak English very well.
:: Eighty percent of Indian households include married couples.

Education: Over 80 percent of Indians in Minnesota are educated professionals who have contributed to the state as doctors, engineers, scientists, and entrepreneurs. Others, including members of the second generation, are making strides in the fields of politics, government, education, media, art, theater, the armed forces, and philanthropy.

Ninety percent of Indians ages twenty-five to sixty-four have a high school diploma. Minnesota's Indians place a high emphasis on education and, like their counterparts in other states, have the highest educational qualifications of all ethnic groups in the United States. Since Indians came to Minnesota to pursue higher education, it is not surprising that over 85 percent of Indian Minnesotans have bachelor's or advanced degrees and over 44 percent have post-graduate or professional degrees. Many of their children, members of the second generation, have followed their parents' footsteps by excelling in school and earning college degrees. Students from India make up the second-largest group of international students in the United States, choosing not just the University of Minnesota but other prestigious institutions, including state and private colleges. Indian students, along with Chinese and South Korean students, account for 57 percent of international students in US universities.

Income Levels: Indian Americans are, by and large, a prosperous immigrant group. They earn the highest median household income: $78,400, compared to $62,700 for all Minnesotans in 2018. The poverty rate for Indian American households is less than six percent compared to 11 percent for all Minnesotans. Indian Americans report the lowest unemployment rate at three percent, compared to five percent for all Minnesotans.

Citizens, Green Card Holders, Temporary Residents: Thirty-five percent of Indian Americans in Minnesota are naturalized citizens. This figure is the lowest among all Asians and may be due to a larger transient population temporarily in the United States for work. Forty-six percent of Minnesota's Indian Americans are homeowners. This figure is also low compared to other Asians and again reflects a population that may be here temporarily.

Businesses: Indian American–owned firms in Minnesota number more than 2,400, had sales of $667 million, and employed more than four thousand people (payroll of $220 million) in 2012 (see "Contributing to Minnesota," pages 116–18).

Family Life: Indian Americans, like most Asians, are family oriented. They tend to view their achievements not as individuals but collectively, as reflections of their families and communities.

According to Pew Research, more than half (54 percent) of Indian Americans say that having a successful marriage is one of the most important things in life; just 34 percent of all American adults agree. Two-thirds of Asian American adults (67 percent) say that being a good parent is one of the most important things in life; just 50 percent of other American adults agree.

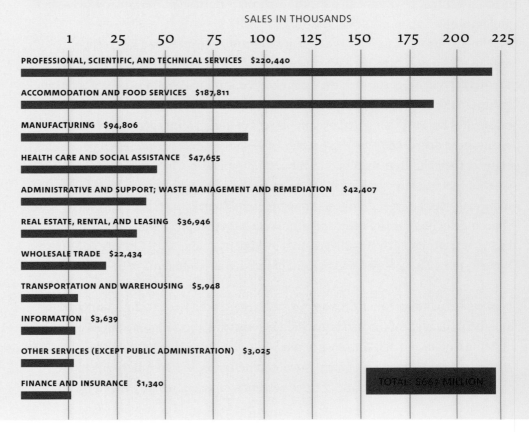

Sales by Indian American Businesses in Minnesota

SALES IN THOUSANDS

	1	25	50	75	100	125	150	175	200	225

PROFESSIONAL, SCIENTIFIC, AND TECHNICAL SERVICES $220,440

ACCOMMODATION AND FOOD SERVICES $187,811

MANUFACTURING $94,806

HEALTH CARE AND SOCIAL ASSISTANCE $47,655

ADMINISTRATIVE AND SUPPORT; WASTE MANAGEMENT AND REMEDIATION $42,407

REAL ESTATE, RENTAL, AND LEASING $36,946

WHOLESALE TRADE $22,434

TRANSPORTATION AND WAREHOUSING $5,948

INFORMATION $3,639

OTHER SERVICES (EXCEPT PUBLIC ADMINISTRATION) $3,025

FINANCE AND INSURANCE $1,340

TOTAL: $667 MILLION

Indian Americans' living arrangements align with these values. They are more likely than all American adults to be married (59 percent vs. 51 percent); their newborns are less likely than all US newborns to have an unmarried mother (16 percent vs. 41 percent); and their children are more likely than all US children to be raised in a household with two married parents (80 percent vs. 63 percent).

Indian Americans are more likely than the general public to live in multigenerational family households. Some 28 percent live with at least two adult generations under the same roof, twice the share of whites and slightly more than the share of blacks and Latinos who live in such households. US Asians also have a strong sense of filial respect; about two-thirds say parents should have a lot or some influence in choosing one's profession (66 percent) and spouse (61 percent).

After this bird's-eye view of Indian Americans in Minnesota, the following pages explore various aspects of this immigrant group's rich and diverse culture and share how its members' many contributions are making a positive impact on Minnesota's landscape.

Given space and time constraints, within these pages only a few selected people and stories represent Minnesota's Indian community. While laying the foundation for future narratives, we hope this first attempt offers readers a good introduction to the Indian American community in Minnesota.

Paramahansa Yogananda with St. Paul Yogoda students during his tour to the Twin Cities in 1927. *MNHS*

Swami Yogananda also offered a series of popular yoga classes. At the end of the course, he received the following commendation signed by the students:

This course of instruction has brought to our minds a world of knowledge not hitherto known to us, making our lives longer and more useful, our minds clearer to receive wisdom, our health more radiant, giving us brighter glimpses of eternity and the things of God. . . . There is no conflict between the Swami's teachings and the Christian religion, as shown by his reverence, faith and eloquent utterances concerning the majesty and glory of the Christian Bible and Jesus Christ. The beautiful spirit here manifested endears him still more to us who have heard his lessons.

2 Coming to Minnesota

In the late nineteenth and early twentieth centuries, job prospects in farming and on railroads, particularly out west, drew the first Indian immigrants from Asia to the United States. However, most early Indians in Minnesota were men who came to study, primarily at the University of Minnesota in engineering and science fields.

The settling of Indian Americans in Minnesota can be traced to three distinct waves. The first wave, arriving before the 1965 Immigration and Nationality Act, included visitors, invited researchers, and a few students. In the second wave, from 1965 through the early 1990s, many came for higher degrees and eventually settled into largely professional jobs; others came to Minnesota after being sponsored by family members. The third wave, from the 1990s to today—marked by preparation for Y2K computer glitches followed by a technology boom—brought thousands of Indians to the United States on H-1B visas; some of them eventually settled in Minnesota.

THE FIRST WAVE (PRE-1965)

The first wave of Indians, mainly visitors, students, and professionals, arrived before the 1965 Immigration and Nationality Act encouraged skilled workers to come to the United States.

Early Visitors

The first real Indian visitor to Minnesota was Paramahansa Yogananda, a Hindu spiritual teacher who visited the state several times to spread the message of kriya yoga, a form of raja-yoga that includes the practice of specific techniques of meditation and spiritual living. Widely known for his best-selling book, *Autobiography*

Minneapolis Daily Star,
September 19, 1927

11

The earliest record of an Indian "stepping" in Minnesota is that of Swami Vivekananda, who came to the United States in 1893 to take part in the World's Parliament of Religions. On his way to Chicago from Vancouver, Canada, on July 30, he briefly stopped at 6:30 AM to switch trains at the St. Paul Union Depot, "touching the soil first time in the USA." *Courtesy Ramakrishna Mission, New Delhi*

of a Yogi, Sri Yogananda founded Self-Realization Fellowship in California in 1920; today the fellowship has more than six hundred temples, centers, and retreats all over the world, including one in Minneapolis established in 1927.

On his first visit to Minnesota in 1927, he stayed three months and gave seventeen free public lectures at Minneapolis's Lyceum Theater (at the site of the current Orchestra Hall). Many advertisements in the *Minneapolis Daily Star* announced his lectures, which were a resounding success, drawing as many as 2,200 audience members.

Early Students

The earliest call for young Indians to study in the United States came in 1902 when Swami Rama Tirtha began touring America to give lectures on Hinduism, survey universities, and seek financial support for visiting students. Swami Rama spent time in Minneapolis lecturing on the need to modernize Indian society through better education and social reform.

The first known student from the subcontinent to enroll at the University of Minnesota was Hira Singh, a Sikh from Lahore, which was then a part of India. Singh was one of the

HINDOO IS HERE TO STUDY MINING

HIGH CASTE NATIVE OF INDIA ENTERS UNIVERSITY.

Is Sent Here as Part of Movement for Higher Education of Natives, Who Are Discouraged by Government— Will Support Himself to Show Countrymen It Can Be Done.

Article about student Hira Singh, in the *Minneapolis Journal*, August 29, 1905

Kokatnur of Bombay, B. A. fr[...] [...]uson College, Poona. M. A. in Ch[...] from University of Minnesota, c[...] Trying for Ph D. in University [...]esota. Obtained fellowship of $50[...]

The *Hindusthanee Student* reported students from India at the University of Minnesota, including, in September 1915, V. Kokatnur (shown) and, in October 1915, A. M. Gurjar. *Courtesy South Asian American Digital Archive (SAADA)*

LEFT Mohan Singh Sekhon graduated from University of Minnesota Medical School. *Courtesy Sylvia Sekhon*

RIGHT Mohan Singh Sekhon with his family, 1950. *Courtesy Sylvia Sekhon*

few Indian men, and later women, who were influenced by Swami Rama to study at the university. He enrolled at the University of Minnesota in 1904 to study mining engineering. According to the *Minneapolis Journal*, "five or six" students also arrived with Hira Singh, and "about twenty more are preparing to come later on." Although Singh was granted a scholarship and was from a well-to-do family, he planned to support himself at the university and was "desiring to show his more timid and less fortunate brethren that the scheme was practicable."

In 1915, a journal for Hindu students in the United States, the *Hindusthanee Times*, listed the University of Minnesota as one of the top American schools for foreign students.

In 1931, another student, eighteen-year-old Mohan Singh Sekhon, came to the United States on a Japanese freighter. He disembarked in Seattle on his way to California, where he had relatives. Admitted to Hamline University, he came to Minnesota to study chemistry. After his graduation in 1934, he attended the University of Minnesota, where he earned a degree in medicine. At that time there were no other Indians in Minnesota, and Dr. Sekhon quickly assimilated into the broader community. He married Margaret Doris Henderson, a Canadian nurse he met at Gillette Hospital. He volunteered as a much-needed doctor for the US Army during World War II. He was stationed in France, close to where his father had served in World War I with the Indian Army. After the war, Dr. Sekhon returned to Minnesota and started a general medical practice in St. Paul at the corner of University and Snelling above a Snyder Brothers drugstore.

He had two children: a daughter, born before he left for the war, and a son, born after he returned. His daughter, Sylvia Sekhon, who retired as a pediatrician in 2018, has treasured all his photographs and memories. She proudly said, "My father felt strongly about giving back to the community that had helped him establish a new life. He volunteered as the health officer for Roseville and Arden Hills and worked hard to bring city water and sewer to both places. He also did school immunizations with the Ramsey County nurses." She added what he'd always reiterated: "This is a good country, but you must work hard to make something of yourself."

In the early years, most Indians seeking higher education abroad came from wealthy families. Before India's independence from the British, most of these students went to the United Kingdom to study in prestigious institutions. Apart from restrictive immigration policies that kept Indians away from US universities, the British also did not allow Indian students to go to the United States, where they might make political trouble by freely spreading nationalist ideas for independence.

After India gained independence in 1947, many Indian students started to consider US colleges and universities for higher degrees. In the 1940s and 1950s, the University of Minnesota invited several Indian students to study, conduct research, and earn their PhDs. Many were from well-off families or had access to information on how to apply to colleges in the United States. As a result, the university's Indian student population rose from ninety-four in 1944 to 1,607 in 1964. While many earned their degrees and then returned to India or took jobs in other states, some decided to settle in Minnesota. Here are stories of a few of these students:

Indru and Dolly Advani. *Courtesy Ramona and Dolly Advani*

Indru and Dolly Advani came to the University of Minnesota as students in 1960, arriving on a cargo-passenger ship, which was the cheapest way to travel. Dolly earned her master's in applied psychology and Indru earned a master of business administration. Since they came from different religious backgrounds—he a Hindu, she a Zoroastrian—there were many objections to their marriage. After Indru's employer sponsored him for permanent residency, they finally married in a civil ceremony in 1963. The wedding was conducted by Judge Rolf Fossen, chief judge for Hennepin County. The Advanis decided to settle in Minnesota and had two children, a son and a daughter. (Their daughter, Ramona Advani, who lives in Minnesota, is a general counsel and deputy state auditor.) Indru had a very successful career as an executive for Blue Cross Blue Shield, and Dolly taught at a nursery school.

Bhupat Desai came to Minnesota in 1963 as a graduate student in industrial engineering at the University of Minnesota. His journey involved almost all modes of transportation: Mumbai to Genoa,

Bhupat and Kumud (Sumita) Desai.
Courtesy Bhupat Desai

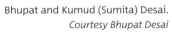

Italy, by ship; Italy to London by train; London to New York by air; and New York to Minneapolis on a Greyhound bus. Desai spent his entire career working for 3M, starting in 1966 and retiring in 2002. He married Kumud (Sumita) in 1967 and settled in St. Paul, where they raised their daughter. The Desais have been active in the Indian community through their involvement in the Gujarati Samaj, in the School of India for Languages and Culture, and in the India Association of Minnesota.

Basant Kharbanda took the initiative of writing to the professors whose textbooks he was studying in his college in India about admission to graduate school in mechanical engineering at the University of Minnesota. He remembered: "I took out a loan to buy a one-way ticket. I arrived in

Basant and Veena Kharbanda.
Courtesy Basant Kharbanda

Minnesota in 1964 with six dollars to my name." He got an assistantship and graduated in 1966, and in 1968 he married Veena during a trip back to India. In 1969, he started a computer company and expanded the business to India in the 1970s. In 1994, he started a real estate business dealing with data centers. The Kharbandas own and manage apartments, hotels, and high-tech real estate.

Mahendra Nath joined the University of Minnesota in August 1964 to pursue a master's degree in industrial engineering. After graduation, he worked at Sperry; while holding down his day job, he started other businesses, including an Indian retail store in Dinkytown, Minneapolis. On a trip to India in 1967, he married Asha, who started selling real estate. In 1985, they established Nath Management, Inc., which over time has included several Burger King franchises and now focuses on managing restaurants, hotels, and real estate. In 2002, Mahendra Nath was inducted into the Minnesota Business Hall of Fame, and he has been featured in *Twin Cites Business Monthly* and in other publications. Mahendra Nath has been a Rotarian for more than thirty-five years.

Mahendra and Asha Nath. *Courtesy Mahendra Nath*

Early Settlers

Other Indians who eventually settled in Minnesota arrived either directly from India or after graduating from colleges and universities in other states and landing jobs in Minnesota. Since there were very few Indians in Minnesota before 1965, most knew each other and assisted one another, irrespective of where they came from in India. Here are their stories:

Patarasp Rustomji Sethna. *Courtesy University of Minnesota Archives, University of Minnesota-Twin Cities*

Patarasp Rustomji Sethna joined the University of Minnesota in 1956 as an associate professor and served as head of the aerospace, engineering, and mechanics department from 1966 to 1992, retiring as professor emeritus in 1993. He passed away in November 1993.

Dr. Padmakar K. Dixit, a biochemist, came to Minnesota directly from India in 1958, when he was offered a job running the anatomy lab at the University of Minnesota. As one of the first Indian families to settle in Minnesota, Padmakar and Vimala Dixit helped many who came after them. They were involved in efforts that helped shape the local Indian community. (One of their daughters, Nayana, and her husband, Ramakrishnan (see page 75), have also contributed to many Indian organizations, including the Hindu temple.)

Sudhanshu Misra, his wife, Induprava (Indu), and their three-year-old daughter, Niru, moved from Cleveland to Minnesota in 1962 after Sudhanshu was offered a job at Honeywell. At that time, he did not even know where Minnesota was located, but six hundred dollars a month was good money then, and the family moved here. Sudhanshu has been an active member of the Indian community, serving as president of the India Association of Minnesota and as a founding member of the 55+ Senior Group, among others, and is a prolific do-it-yourself-er. Indu was one of the first Indian women to attend college in Minnesota; she earned a

Dr. Padmakar K. and Vimala Dixit. *Courtesy Nayana Ramakrishnan*

Indu, Niru, and Sudhanshu Misra. *Courtesy Niru Misra*

graduate degree in social work and started a business in Minneapolis, Hati House, a residential program for chemically dependent people, which their daughter Niru is now running. (Niru Misra also has served as president of the India Association of Minnesota and has been involved in other Indian organizations.)

Pennamma Jacob arrived in the United States in 1959 to study at the St. Joseph School of Nursing in Marshfield, Wisconsin. Only sixteen years old, she had barely ever left the small town in Kerala, India, where she was born when she boarded a plane with her sister, Allie, who was eighteen. At twenty-five, in a match arranged by relatives, Pennamma married Kurian Cherucheril in Minnesota and they settled here, raising three children, a son and two daughters. Both retired from long careers spent at one place—she from nursing at Fairview Hospital and he from teaching chemistry at Cretin-Derham Hall High School.

Pennamma Jacob and her sister arrived in Stevens Point, Wisconsin, where they were received by nursing school director Sister Edith. *Courtesy Pennamma Cherucheril*

Jagadish Desai. *Courtesy Jagadish Desai*

After graduating with a degree in chemical engineering from Montana State University in 1962, *Jagadish Desai* borrowed a hundred dollars from his fiancée, Roswitha, flipped a coin on which way to go, and headed to Minneapolis in a beat-up old car. Just before running out of money, he found a job at the battery company Gould. He and Roswitha were married later that year in St. Paul. A founding member of the India Club, Jagadish was actively involved in the Indian community in the early days and was instrumental in connecting the community with several institutions in which he held leadership positions. Jagadish earned a law degree and practiced law until he retired in 2001.

Professor K. S. P. Kumar joined the University of Minnesota's electrical engineering department in 1964 after earning his PhD from Purdue University. He was encouraged to apply to US colleges by two visiting professors who came to his college in India in 1958. As a graduate student, he was an intern at Honeywell in Minneapolis; he then sought employment at the University of Minnesota.

In 1968, he returned to India to get married. He and his wife, Usha (a founding member of the School of India for Languages

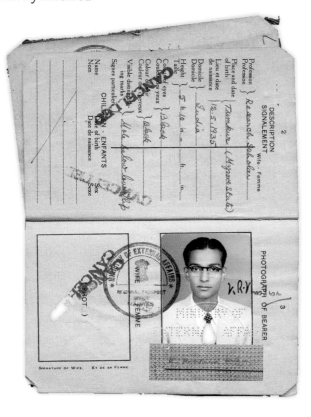

K. S. P. Kumar's passport; he became a professor of electrical and computer engineering. *Courtesy Professor K. S. P. Kumar*

and Culture), settled in Minnesota and raised two boys who both became professors (one son, Satish Kumar, is at the University of Minnesota as a Distinguished University McKnight Professor of chemical engineering and materials science). Besides his teaching career, Kumar has been a prolific speaker for thirty-five years, giving discourses on Hinduism at the Hindu temple and at local schools and churches. He retired as professor emeritus in 2003.

Sant Ram Arora came to the United States in 1958 and earned his PhD from Johns Hopkins University. He came to Minnesota in 1964 when he was offered a job as an

associate professor in the industrial engineering department. On a visit to India, he married Sudha; they settled in Minnesota, where they raised three children. He was actively involved in the Geeta Ashram and mentored several Indian students majoring in industrial engineering. Sant retired as professor emeritus in 2012 after fifty years of teaching and passed away on April 12, 2018.

Sant Ram and Sudha Arora in New Delhi, departing for the United States. *Courtesy Sudha Arora*

Ram Gada came to Minnesota in 1964 to work for a consulting engineering firm after receiving his master's degree in mechan-

ical engineering from North Dakota State University. In 1967, he got permanent residency and returned to India to marry Neena. They settled in Minnesota, where they raised their daughter and son. (Daughter Lisa is a real estate agent in Wayzata.) Gada started his own consulting engineering firm in 1980, which he ran until he retired in 2010.

Gada has been a stalwart of the Indian community, providing leadership to and assistance with many organizations. As an early settler, he was a founding member of several organizations: Gujarati Samaj, Jain Center, and the Minnesota Asian Indian Democratic Association (MAIDA). Ram has been actively involved in the School of India for Languages and Culture (Neena was one of the founding members), Hindu Mandir, and SEWA–Asian Indian

Ram and Neena Gada.
Courtesy Ram Gada

Family Wellness (SEWA-AIFW) and is an honorary advisor to the India Association of Minnesota board. Ram has also worked extensively with the Minnesota Historical Society, initiating oral history projects and the *Beyond Bollywood* exhibit for the Indian community. He is often invited to speak on Jainism and has helped raise funds for many organizations and causes.

Sy Mody came to Minnesota in 1965 to join 3M after graduating with a degree in industrial engineering from the University of North Dakota. In 1967 he returned to

India to marry Kokila, and they settled in Minnesota, where they raised two girls (thirty-five years of their life here were focused on the care of daughter Seema, who had special needs). Kokila ran a home-based business, and Sy was involved in the India Club, the Hindu Society, and Gujarati Samaj. He retired from 3M in 2000, after thirty-five years of service.

Sy and Kokila Mody.
Courtesy Sy Mody

Kalyanji and Vimla Patel came to Minnesota when Kalyanji landed a job at 3M. The two had met and married in Pennsylvania while Vimla was studying psychology at Temple University in 1957. In those days, it was rare for single women to leave India to study. The Patels raised three boys in Minnesota. As a Sanskrit scholar, Vimla is well versed in Hindu scriptures and volunteered at the Geeta Ashram. Kalyanji passed away in 1993.

Dr. Varanasi Rama Murthy joined the University of Minnesota in 1965 after earning his PhD in geology from Yale in 1957. In his long and illustrious career as a geochemist and geophysicist, he held various administrative roles at the University of Minnesota, including vice provost, associate vice president, and interim president. He died on October 12, 2012, in California at the age of seventy-nine.

Others who came:
:: Vasant Kolpe
:: Dr. Naresh and Kusum Jain
:: Sharad Bhatt
:: MJ Abhishekar

THE SECOND WAVE (1965–1990)

The Civil Rights Act of 1964 prompted immigration reform, and a year later President Lyndon Johnson signed the Immigration and Nationality Act of 1965. This act ended the quota system based on national origins and established a new immigration policy designed to attract skilled labor to the United States. It also included provisions for reuniting immigrant families. The passage of this act led to many students coming to Minnesota for higher education. A large group of students arrived in 1967, followed by many more in 1969 and 1973, and a steady stream thereafter.

Many of these students were from educated and middle- to upper-middle-class families and were among the first to go abroad. These students, especially those with undergraduate degrees in science and engineering, were awarded scholarships and assistantships, but others had to borrow money or take out loans. Newly independent India was not an open economy, and in the 1960s and 1970s the Reserve Bank of India granted only eight dollars' worth of foreign exchange. Most of these students

When students departed to the United States for "higher studies," as it was called, large groups of family and friends came to send them off with the traditional garland of flowers. Freelance photographers did brisk business by taking memorable pictures of these gatherings.

ABOVE LEFT Anoop Mathur at Santa Cruz Airport, Bombay, with his aunt, uncle, and cousin just before his departure on August 16, 1973. *Courtesy Anoop Mathur*

ABOVE RIGHT Family and friends from Bada village came to the Bombay seaport to bid farewell to Ram Gada, who left for the the United States to pursue a master of science degree on Sunday, February 9, 1964, via SS *Chusan. Courtesy Ram Gada*

started their lives in the United States with this meager amount and had to plan carefully until money from their assistantships or bank loans and other sources came through.

Almost all students expected that their stay would be temporary, but the prospect of good jobs and a good life persuaded them to settle in the United States. India had limited job opportunities at the time; the few who returned had family businesses or other responsibilities. During this period when so many Indian Americans decided to stay in the United States, the term *brain drain* was used to describe the phenomenon of members of this talented pool not returning to India.

For Indian students graduating with higher and professional degrees, the Immigration and Nationality Act opened new opportunities for working and settling in Minnesota. With specialized degrees in technology, science, and medicine in hand, many were hired by large companies such as 3M, Honeywell, Control Data, Pillsbury, Cargill, Medtronic, IBM, and the University of Minnesota as well as by Mayo Clinic and other local hospitals and research institutions. A few were hired by small technology businesses, where they quickly rose through the ranks.

To retain these highly talented workers, employers sponsored them for green cards (permanent resident cards), which allowed them to stay in the United States indefinitely. While in the sixties it was

In the 1960s, several United States Information Services (USIS) centers were set up in large cities in India. The *Peterson's Guide* to US graduate schools was in high demand in these centers from students applying to American universities. Students from well-known Indian colleges such as the Indian Institute of Technology (IIT) were readily accepted because American professors were already familiar with their schools' curriculum.

Three of Minnesota's Indian American families are featured in *The $8 Man: From India to North America, Immigrants Who Came with Nothing and Changed Everything*, edited by Brenda H. Christensen: *Gummadi and Shirley Franklin*, for founding PUSHPA (see page 75); *Ram and Neena Gada*, for community building and assimilation; and *Ram and Nayana Ramakrishnan*, for water harvesting projects in India.

Things They Carried

Travel experts advise to pack light. But how do you pack when you are leaving the comforts of your home and may not be back for awhile?

Although baggage allowances in early years were more lenient than now, two suitcases was still the maximum. Most Indians who came to the United States in the 1960s and '70s, when Indian groceries were not widely available, always packed some staples such as lentils, special spices, and Indian pickles. The latter created a niche business in India—to vacuum-seal pickles so they pass US customs and do not leak in suitcases!

Women always bring Indian clothing and jewelry to wear to Indian events. Newlyweds often pack a few of their wedding presents, and everyone brings gifts for colleagues and neighbors.

When space and weight allow, travelers bring books, family recipes, cooking utensils, and photographs of special memories. In the past, many packed cassette tapes and even vinyl records of favorite music.

Suitcase display from *Beyond Bollywood* exhibit. *MNHS.*

relatively easy to get green cards, the recession of 1973–75 threw the status of many Indians into limbo. Job offers became scarce and sponsorships declined. When the relationship between US president Richard Nixon and Indian prime minister Indira Gandhi soured, the situation worsened for students who were admitted to the University of Minnesota. Bilateral exchanges were canceled, and financial assistantships were withdrawn.

Encouraged by the family reunification provision in the 1965 Immigration Act, Indian Americans in Minnesota sponsored immediate family members, including parents and siblings, to become permanent residents. As more and more Indians of all ages and educational levels arrived, organizations and businesses were established to meet the needs of a diverse and growing population.

In 1980, the first year in which the federal census included the category of Asian Indians, the population of Indian Americans in Minnesota was estimated to be 3,670. By 1990, it had grown to about 8,234.

Many Indian organizations were established in the 1970s, 1980s, and 1990s, including the India Club, later renamed the India Association of Minnesota (IAM), as well as several religious and regional organizations.

When he applied for a teaching job at the University of Minnesota in 1964, K. P. S. Kumar recollects, "I came here on a Friday for an interview, was offered a position on Monday and by the following Monday, I was in Minnesota. It was so easy then."

No Domestic Help?

For students, particularly the men who arrived in the 1960s and '70s, balancing studying with cooking their meals and cleaning their apartments was a great burden. Many came from upper-middle-class families in India who most likely had maids and cooks to do this work. Despite the availability of dishwashers, vacuum cleaners, and washing machines, home chores were still something to complain about. Today, while it is more common to hire cleaning services and outsource other tasks, chores remain a topic of hot discussion, especially whenever someone new arrives or after returning from a trip to India.

The International Students Office and Host Families

Host families and the International Students Office, primarily at the University of Minnesota, played critical roles in many Indian students' lives, particularly those who came in the 1960s and early 1970s. The office provided a much-needed venue for students to meet each other, learn about available facilities, get help with visas and work permits, and, most of all, have a familiar, comfortable place to hang out.

One memorable undertaking from the early days was that the office offered to record and mail cassette tapes of students talking to their families. At a time when making a phone call was unaffordable, this help was invaluable. Others recalled that when student died the office helped with the expense of transporting the body or remains back to India.

Several Minnesota families signed up to host international students and provided essential support to Indian students. These families were usually the first contact for the students, receiving them at the airport, helping them settle in, and guiding them in understanding American life and culture. When most American students went home for Thanksgiving and Christmas holidays, these families opened their homes and included the students in their gatherings. Strong bonds developed between the students and their host families, and after graduating and settling down in Minnesota, many of these former students reciprocated by inviting the host families to their own homes and to their celebrations.

Foreign students with advisor Joseph Mestenhauser (left), 1959. *Courtesy University of Minnesota Archives, University of Minnesota–Twin Cities*

Myrna Peterson, who befriended the Misra family, ran a boardinghouse near the University of Minnesota's St. Paul campus. Over the years, at least twenty Indian graduate students lived with her. Niru Misra, who had come to Minnesota as a three-year-old, recalled: "She was like a mother to the students and a grandmother to me. The word *help* seems inadequate to describe the support she provided. When nobody had any family members in those days, her care for us was invaluable." *Courtesy Niru Misra*

In 1962, Dr. Dixit was having lunch at the University of Minnesota when he heard someone say, "*Namastay,* how are you?" in Hindi. The silver-haired woman was Margaret Grainger. Grainger, the daughter of missionaries, had lived in India until she was seventeen, and she provided tremendous help and support to the newly arrived family. "From showing how to use laundry machines to buying groceries, she was our go-to person during those early years and part of all our celebrations all through her life," recalls Nayana (Dixit) Ramakrishnan. *Courtesy Nayana Ramakrishnan*

Darlene Sheeso, shown here with husband Sherman, introduced Indian students to Minnesota activities in the 1970s. *Courtesy Darlene Sheeso*

The Third Wave (1990s–2000s)

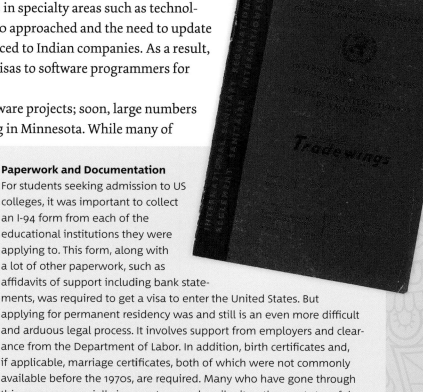

Vaccination certificate.
Courtesy Anoop Mathur

The US Immigration Act of 1990 created the H-1B visa, which temporarily employed highly skilled, college-educated foreign workers in specialty areas such as technology, medicine, and the sciences. As the year 2000 approached and the need to update computer programs grew, this task was outsourced to Indian companies. As a result, the government granted several hundred H-1B visas to software programmers for work in high tech companies in Minnesota.

These workers' success led to additional software projects; soon, large numbers of skilled computer professionals began arriving in Minnesota. While many of them remained only for the duration of a project, others were able to change their visa status to permanent residency. In 2000, the Indian population in Minnesota was 19,963. By 2010, it doubled to 38,097, and by 2017, it reached 43,379.

This influx of both temporary and permanent Indian Americans changed the landscape of Indian American businesses and organizations. Several Indian grocery stores and Indian restaurants opened. IndiaFest, organized by IAM and held in August each year, grew large enough to move from the Landmark Center in St. Paul to the grounds of the capitol mall.

Paperwork and Documentation

For students seeking admission to US colleges, it was important to collect an I-94 form from each of the educational institutions they were applying to. This form, along with a lot of other paperwork, such as affidavits of support including bank statements, was required to get a visa to enter the United States. But applying for permanent residency was and still is an even more difficult and arduous legal process. It involves support from employers and clearance from the Department of Labor. In addition, birth certificates and, if applicable, marriage certificates, both of which were not commonly available before the 1970s, are required. Many who have gone through this process, especially in recent years, describe it as the most stressful part of deciding to live in the United States.

Additional regional and religious institutions were established, each catering to different linguistic regions, spiritual practices, and their subsects. Many other places of worship, performing arts organizations, and bands and music groups were established, and businesses such as clothing boutiques, caterers, and tailors began to offer their services. By 2018, the India Association of Minnesota recorded more than fifty India-related organizations.

Indian Diaspora

Not all Indian Americans in Minnesota came directly from India. Many came from other countries their ancestors had migrated to from India. Others were children adopted from India, while still others were either born in India or lived there with their missionary parents. Here is a look at the Indian diaspora in Minnesota.

Indo-Caribbean and Malaysian

Many Minnesotans of Indian origin came from former British island colonies such as Trinidad, Fiji, Guyana, and Malaysia, where their ancestors had either been sent as indentured workers and laborers in the late 1800s or were hired by the British to manage plantations.

While the Malaysian Indians occasionally meet socially, they have largely assimilated with other Indians in Minnesota. On the other hand, the Indo-Caribbean Indians have, for the most part, maintained their own identity by creating different organizations and places of worship. Here are profiles of a few members of this group.

Harry Singh, born in Trinidad and Tobago, came to Minnesota in 1970 to study at St. Thomas University. His great-grandparents were from India, and his mother's cooking displayed strong Indian influences. In 1983, he and his wife, Ann Marie Singh, opened a restaurant on Nicollet Avenue's Eat Street in Minneapolis. Harry Singh's Original Caribbean Restaurant is still a popular destination for those craving hot and spicy Indo-Caribbean food.

Ramraj Singh, one of the early immigrants from Guyana, came to Minnesota to attend college; he retired as director of community education. People like him, descendants of Indians who hail from Guyana, still maintain very close ties with the Indian way of life. Many in Minnesota are Hindus and have established temples of their own. While early immigrants from these countries may have held mostly blue-collar jobs, the pattern has been changing as members of the second generation set their sights on Ivy League colleges as an avenue to more prestigious employment and higher incomes.

Lily Tharoor, who came to Minnesota via Houston, was born in Singapore, which was then part of Malaysia. While her mother was born there, her father arrived in Malaysia as a nineteen-year-old to earn money to send back to his family in India. He worked in a clinic for a rubber plantation and quickly rose to become head of human resources. Lily says, "My father was a strong believer in education; he sent all his kids—my brothers and me—to the US for higher studies." Lily is a social worker for St. Paul Public Schools and lives in St. Paul with her husband, Kurt Johnston.

Anantanand Rambachan, a professor of religion, philosophy, and Asian studies at St. Olaf College since 1985, was born in Trinidad. Both his grandparents were Hindu priests, and as a Hindu, he is the first non-Christian to serve as the chair of his department. Professor Rambachan has been involved in promoting interreligious discourses and has authored several books about Hinduism. In 2003 and 2004, he was invited to deliver the invocation at the White House celebration of Diwali, the Hindu festival of lights.

East Africans

Another set of Indian immigrants who came to Minnesota are from East Africa—from Uganda, Tanzania, and Kenya.

Indians moved to East Africa in the 1890s to work on British-run infrastructure projects. By the 1970s, many of their descendants had become quite successful, owning businesses that employed Africans and held immense economic and social clout. However, after African countries gained independence, Indians began to lose status. Citizens of the newly independent nations, resentful of the Indians and their privileged positions, inflicted discriminatory rules that forced many Indians to leave their longtime homes.

In 1972, President Idi Amin of Uganda expelled that nation's Indian minority, giving them only ninety days to leave. Many who held British passports settled in the United Kingdom; others found their way to far-flung parts of the world. Sponsored by Lutheran World Federation, ten Ugandan families came to Minnesota and restarted their lives.

Many Indians in Tanzania also chose to leave the country after facing widespread discrimination and when their properties and businesses were being expropriated after nationalization. Similarly, Indians in Kenya faced hostility and discrimination after the country became independent. They were not granted citizenship and had to stand in lines each year to renew their residency status.

Ramnik Shah was a prominent accountant with many important clients from President Idi Amin's government in Uganda when he was forced to leave the country. He lived in London for a while before moving to Winnipeg, Canada. Ramnik and his family arrived in Minnesota in 1980, sponsored by his wife's sister. After briefly working for an accounting company, he started his own firm, which has been very successful with several international business clients. Ramnik and his wife, Susheela, have stayed connected with other Indians in Minnesota and have been active with the India Association of Minnesota. (His son, Dr. Rajiv Shah, started Athletes Committed to Educating Students [ACES], a Twin Cities organization that helps to reduce the academic gap among underserved students [see page 100].)

A dare from her friends inspired *June Noronha* to enter the US information office in Nairobi to ask for information on applying for colleges in the United States. Admitted to Macalester College, she arrived in August 1967, hot and uncomfortable in a pink woolen suit that was made with Minnesota winter in mind. Born and raised in Kenya by parents who moved there from India, she looked Indian but knew

Professor Anantanand Rambachan

barely enough to respond to questions about her ancestral home. After graduation, with her US visa running out, she found herself close to becoming stateless. She could not return to Kenya because she had failed to register when she had turned twenty-one, and although she held a UK passport, she was not accepted there either. On the eve of her US visa expiring, a sponsorship recommendation from Minnesota Senator Hubert Humphrey saved her from being deported to an internment camp in the United Kingdom.

> **Several others of Indian descent** held jobs or encountered circumstances that took them to countries such as Pakistan or Canada or in the Middle East or Europe before they landed in the United States and in Minnesota

Noronha has taught at St. Catherine University, has worked for the Bush Foundation, and is now an executive coach. She has won many awards for her efforts on internationalism and human rights, including Macalester's distinguished citizen award, and she was named one of one hundred most influential women by St. Kate's.

Adopted Indian Children

Many children who were born in India arrived in Minnesota when they were adopted by non-Indian Americans through various agencies. (Indian American families have also adopted children from India; their transition and upbringing have been similar to that of other second-generation Indians.) Many of the children who were adopted in the early 1980s quickly assimilated into life in their adopted country, losing touch with their Indian roots. But others who came in the 1990s and later were able to maintain links to their Indian heritage through their parents' extensive efforts and organizations such as Holt International. Several of these children attended the School of India for Languages and Culture (SILC) in St. Paul.

In addition, Parents of Indian Children (PIC), later renamed Programs for Indian Children, with assistance from SILC, Pangea World Theater, India Association of Minnesota, and many volunteer members of the Indian community, and through cultural camps and get-togethers, helped these children stay in touch with Indian culture. In recent years, such activities are held at the Children's Home Society in St. Paul and at adoptive family gatherings.

Camp Masala, held on the University of St. Thomas campus on Father's Day weekend, draws many adopted and blended families not only from Minnesota but also from other states such as Alaska and Wisconsin.

Leah Roberts was adopted in 1989 by a Jewish couple who were both doctors. She grew up mostly around people of Jewish faith. Except for two girls at the synagogue who were also adopted from India, Leah had no exposure to Indians. After she started a senior support business called Grandmother's Helper, she began to meet Indians through her clients. Leah remembers her very loving and happy childhood, but she also wishes she had learned more about her Indian heritage and hopes to expose her children to that cultural grounding.

Anil Ramer was a year old when he was adopted from India by Rob Ramer and Deborah McLaren. Rob had been born in India to medical missionary parents, and Deborah was a sustainable tourism specialist who had worked extensively in the Himalayas. Adopting a child from India was a natural choice for them. However, the adoption process became mired in politics between the Indian government and the orphanage where Anil was born. After much support from Minnesota Senator Paul Wellstone, hundreds of letters from Indian community members, and Rob and Deborah moving to India to ensure his safe and legal adoption, Anil finally could come to Minnesota.

Anil Ramer at Mysore Palace, India. *Courtesy Deborah McLaren*

Rob and Deborah feel strongly that it is important for adoptive families to maintain a connection to their child's original homeland. Thus, right from the beginning, Anil was exposed to Indian culture, first through his father's extended Minnesota family (which included other Indians), and later through the efforts of both of his parents through the India culture camps that Deborah helped organize. They also traveled to India, which the family considers their other home country.

Anil is a student at St. Paul College and has a diverse group of friends. He is also involved with the family's Indian spice business and has been learning to prepare Indian cuisine and helping create various spice blends.

Children of Missionaries

Yet another group of people who have contributed to the Indian diaspora in Minnesota are children of missionaries who went to India. Although they may not look like Indians, they were either born in India or spent their formative years there. When they returned to the United States and to Minnesota, they identified strongly with India, spoke an Indian language, and were accustomed to Indian culture and food.

The Ramer family in Sangli, Maharashtra, India, 1964. *Courtesy Jody Chrastek*

Henry and Dolores Scholberg regularly attended gatherings of the 55+, an Indian senior group, in the 1990s. *Courtesy Sudhanshu Misra*

Many got involved with Indian organizations and socialized among Indians. In Minnesota, there are about fifty to seventy-five people who were children of missionaries in India, and many attended Woodstock, an international school in Mussoorie, Uttarakhand, India, that was popular with the missionaries.

Bob and Nancy Ramer met in India, where they were working in mission programs, he as an engineer teaching trade school and she as a public health nurse. Three of their four children were born there. Two of those children, Jody Chrastek and Rob Ramer, live in Minnesota now. Both have been involved with the Indian community in the Twin Cities. Jody taught preschool at School of India for Languages and Culture and adopted an Indian child, now an adult. A pediatric hospice nurse, she travels to India frequently to train and to share her experience with palliative care. Rob served on the India Association of Minnesota board; he and his wife have also adopted a son from India. Jody recalls, "My brothers and I were called 'white Indians'!"

Henry Scholberg, who was the director and librarian of the Ames Library of South Asia at the University of Minnesota, was born in Darjeeling, India, in 1921 to parents who were Methodist missionaries. Henry spoke Hindi before he learned to speak English and was influenced by the peaceful acts of Mahatma Gandhi. Scholberg returned to the United States in 1939 to attend the University of Illinois, graduating in 1943. He earned his master's in library science in 1962 from the University of Minnesota and was the first director of the newly established Ames Library, from which he retired in 1986. He was a prolific author and wrote several books and plays set in India. During his time at the library, he befriended many Indian students who regularly came to read Indian newspapers and magazines. He passed away in August 2012 after suffering head injuries from a cycling accident.

3 Settling Down, Adapting, and Assimilating

Once Indians decided to work and live in Minnesota, they had to choose where to buy houses and start the process of adapting and assimilating in their new homeland.

SETTLEMENT PATTERNS

When Indians first started arriving in Minnesota, they chose to live in and around the Twin Cities campuses of the University of Minnesota. In the late 1960s and early 1970s, Indian Americans with full-time jobs and permanent resident visas began buying houses and settling down. Many chose the Twin Cities suburbs, particularly ones with reputations for good schools with high academic standards.

Eighty-three percent of Indian Americans in Minnesota live in the suburbs of the Twin Cities, while 17 percent live outside the Twin Cities, including a contingent near Moorhead. In the 1970s and 1980s, a sizeable percentage of Indians lived in the suburbs of New Brighton and Bloomington. By 2010, the suburbs of Eden Prairie, Edina, Maple Grove, Plymouth, Wayzata, and Woodbury saw significant growth, with 32 percent of the state's Indian population living in the southwestern suburbs. In 2018, Eden Prairie had the largest number of Indian Americans: more than five percent out of the city's total population of 61,000 were Indian American. Certain neighborhoods have such a high concentration of Indian Americans that almost every other house is owned by an Indian. Suburbs such as Plymouth host summer picnics and other special gatherings to bring together all local Indians.

Since Indian Americans also belong to a group of immigrants with high median income, affluent areas such as Edina, Minnetonka, North Oaks, Orono, and Wayzata also include many Indian American families.

With the introduction of H-1B visas and the arrival of temporary workers in computer and software fields starting in 2000, Indian families have completely

Where Indian Americans Live in Minnesota

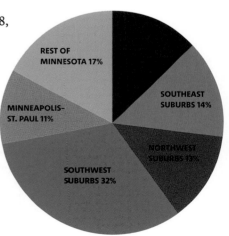

REST OF MINNESOTA 17%

SOUTHEAST SUBURBS 14%

MINNEAPOLIS–ST. PAUL 11%

NORTHWEST SUBURBS 13%

SOUTHWEST SUBURBS 32%

Making Minnesota Home

In 1953, Dr. Mohan Sekhon bought land on the shore of Lake Johanna in Arden Hills and had a house built for his family. The original house still stands, although it has been remodeled and renovated. His daughter, Sylvia, remembers that Dr. Sekhon would sit outside by the lake and quote, in Persian, words that the seventeenth-century Mughal Emperor Jahangir uttered when he visited the beautiful Kashmir valley in India:

Gar firdaus bar-rue zamin ast, hami asto, hamin asto, hamin ast.

If there is a heaven on earth, it's this, it's this, none but this.

Dixit home. *Courtesy author*

The Dixit family bought their house in southeast Minneapolis, close to the University of Minnesota, in 1962. For many years, the house served as a home-away-from-home for students and newcomers from India. It is often on the must-make-a-stop list for visitors who experienced the Dixits' hospitality during their student days.

The Misra family bought their first house in 1963 in northeast Minneapolis. Like the Dixits, the Misras generously opened their home to many new people from India.

Other early settlers, such as the Mangalick family, maintained an open and welcoming home, as did those who had come to Minnesota as students and then settled down. Many went out of the way to welcome and help newcomers, particularly students.

occupied several apartment complexes. One of these buildings in Hopkins has acquired the nickname of "Ramsgate," playing on a Hindu deity's name, because of the number of Indians renting the units.

Among Indians living outside the Twin Cities, Rochester leads with six percent of its population being Indian. This concentration is largely due to the number of Indian doctors and engineers employed at the Mayo Clinic and at IBM, respectively. In the early years, many Indians living in this area would make frequent trips to the Twin Cities for groceries and to attend concerts or religious activities. However, by 2018, the significant population encouraged the opening of at least two Indian grocery stores and the establishment of a Hindu temple and the Rochester Indian Community Association of Minnesota, which provides a platform for all Indian subpopulations in the greater Rochester area. Also, due to this growth, visiting Indian artists are beginning to include Rochester in their itineraries.

The population in other areas such as Duluth, Mankato, Osseo, and St. Cloud each reportedly have at least one percent Indians. St. Cloud State University is home to the India Heritage Club.

ASSIMILATING AND ADAPTING

> "What did I bring with me to Minnesota? First, I brought my accent. I also brought the hopes and dreams of my family and community, and their anxieties—will my son come back?"
> Raj Menon, 2015

Moving to another country with a different culture is difficult, especially during the early years of the transition. Indian pioneers who arrived before the internet era made information readily available and who had to navigate a new life without help from friends and family faced tough years. Minnesota's harsh winters and lack of Indian groceries, familiar foods, and places to worship coupled with new social and cultural norms proved challenging.

However, as years went by, Indians began to assimilate

Living in a Small Town

Dr. Venkata Krishna Murthy and his wife, Kamakshi, have lived in Sleepy Eye, Minnesota, for more than thirty-seven years.

Dr. Murthy came to the United States in 1963 from a small village in Tamil Nadu, India, to complete his surgical residency. The family moved from Pennsylvania to Mora, Minnesota, in 1972 and then, in 1982, to Sleepy Eye, where they raised three children, including a daughter with hearing impairment. All three children attended local schools, have built successful careers, and live in different parts of the United States.

At first, being the only Indians in town was challenging. Making the 125-mile, one-way trip to the Twin Cities for Indian groceries and for social, cultural, and religious events was an added burden but is now part of the routine. Sometimes, the Murthys even drive to the Twin Cities twice a week to see friends or to volunteer at the temple.

After living in Sleepy Eye for so long, they have become an integral part of the community. Dr. Murthy continues his work as a surgeon at the local hospital as well as in neighboring towns. Kamakshi is an active volunteer and community member. Both travel extensively to see their children and five grandchildren and to visit lifelong friends.

Kamakshi Murthy (left) volunteers weekly at a food shelf in Sleepy Eye, Minnesota, where she also serves as a board member. She volunteers at Trinity Church, helping make quilts to send to disaster-stricken areas. Each year the church group makes about 320 quilts, which are distributed from a center in Minneapolis. *Courtesy Kamakshi Murthy*

Dolly Advani takes an oath of allegiance at a naturalization ceremony. Only 23 percent of Indian Americans settled in Minnesota are nationalized citizens. *Courtesy Ramona and Dolly Advani*

Of non-Indians who have married Indians, many have become part of the Indian community by socializing with its members, and a few have even become involved in Indian organizations, volunteering and providing leadership.

Har Shukla, retired from corporate life, writes poems in Hindi on Minnesota and his life here.

*Rum aur Mississippi ka sangam kuch khadmon hi aagey hai
Rum miltay hi Mississippi bhi itlati balkati hai*

The confluence of Rum River and Mississippi River is but a step away [from my home in Anoka].
No sooner Rum River meets the Mississippi, the latter dances away with many twists and turns.

Hold the Hamburger: Food Challenges

In the 1960s and 1970s, vegetarian food (forget vegan or gluten-free) was not often a menu option in restaurants and cafeterias. Many vegetarians went hungry or lived on French fries when they had to eat outside their home. Some recall the surprised look on the cashier's face when they would order a fast-food hamburger but ask to hold the hamburger patty.

Indians who do not eat beef or pork had limited choices when dining out. For those unfamiliar with typical midwestern fare, standing in a cafeteria line and trying to decide what to order was and continues to be nerve-racking. Pizza is a popular choice, and sometimes Chinese or Mexican foods. In recent years dining options have become more satisfying thanks to the growing variety of Indian and other ethnic restaurants in Minnesota.

into their new lives. For early settlers, often there wasn't a choice; opportunities in India were limited, and since they had made the decision to relocate in Minnesota and had taken all the risks, it was important to adapt and learn to straddle the two cultures. The process for immigrants with non-Indian spouses was faster as they had help to assimilate and blend quickly.

Adapting to Minnesota's winters: baby's day out (*Sudha Arora*); snowshoeing and snow blowing (*author*)

From buying houses—and learning to mow lawns and shovel snow—to getting involved in their children's schools, volunteering in the community, and enjoying the American way of life, Indians began to change. Many, if not all, learned to participate in a broad range of activities.

Along with keeping up with academics, many Indians, especially the second generation, participate in sports such as baseball, tennis, and soccer. Avid sports fans enthusiastically attend and watch games. Others, especially retirees, belong to bridge clubs. Many spend summer months teeing off for a game of golf.

Many Indians are also involved in mainstream activities such going to movies, museums, and concerts, trying out new cuisines and restaurants, or traveling and taking road trips. Some have embraced the outdoors and Minnesota life, pursuing activities such as camping, canoeing, fishing, skiing, snowshoeing, and snow tubing.

Come Again?
Despite polished English skills and excellent scores on their Test of English as a Foreign Language (TOEFL), many Indians, especially the ones who arrived before the internet era, are stumped when they first encounter typical American expressions such as "come again?"—for when people do not understand them—or "up the creek without a paddle," or "I plead the Fifth." But as they assimilate, they become comfortable not only with American slang but also with corporate speak. Then it all becomes *doable*, as they even use *wanna* and *gonna* in their conversations.

The Indian community in the United States is unique in that many people are here temporarily on work assignments. In 2016, Indians were the top recipients of high-skilled H-1B temporary visas. This group, popularly referred to as "H-1B people" or "software people" because of their visas and their jobs in the software industry, has changed Minnesota's Indian community since they first started arriving toward the end of the 1990s. Because of this large influx, demand for Indian grocery stores, restaurants, and other services has grown. While not all participate in mainstream activities, their presence is seen at Indian grocery stores, in places of worship, and in events organized by Indian groups.

Road trip to a farm in Red Wing and Lake Pepin, 1964. *Courtesy Niru Misra*

Enjoying Minnesota's lakes, with typical Indian hospitality. *Courtesy author*

Catch of the day. *Courtesy author*

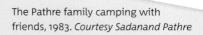

The Pathre family camping with friends, 1983. *Courtesy Sadanand Pathre*

Family reunion, Minnesota style: the Namboodri clan (originally from Kerala, India) go camping and hiking for their annual gatherings. *Courtesy Godan Nambudiripad*

Shanti Shah and Stephen Peterson rented an RV to take Shanti's family on a tour of national parks. The RV's kitchen was used to cook meals to accommodate the family's strict dietary needs, which would have been difficult to manage in hotels and motels. *Courtesy Shanti Shah*

4 Preserving Culture, Heritage, Family Values, and Traditions

While Indian Americans have assimilated well into the broader Minnesota community, taking part in many aspects of national and regional culture, they have also held on to their Indian traditions through language, food, and celebrations and by establishing cultural and religious organizations. While this emphasis on culture may be changing with the second generation, the early settlers have retained many of their original values and traditions and have also maintained strong ties with the country of their birth.

FAMILY LIFE

Like most Asians, Indians are very family oriented. Although the attitude of the second generation may be shifting, relationships and a sense of self tend to be less individualistic and more family centric. While not very common, a few children live with their parents even after getting married, and many homes have three generations living under one roof.

Visiting India and Inviting Family for Visits

For many Indians in Minnesota, going back to India to visit family is a much anticipated and, indeed, required part of living here. To plan for these visits means saving not only money but also vacation time. In the early years, when ticket prices were not commensurate with salaries, a trip to India was not very affordable and could be planned only every three to four years. In recent years, as ticket prices have remained stable, travel has become more affordable and some make it back to India annually. Many retired Indians in particular escape Minnesota winters and explore destination sites in India that they could not visit during their working years.

Before the multigeneration home trend caught on in Minnesota, a few Indian families were building or buying homes with independent units for parents; some were even equipped with kitchens and separate entrances. Lisa Norton, a second-generation Indian, and her husband, Thomas, bought their house in Minnetonka with independent living quarters below so that Lisa's parents, Ram and Neena Gada, could move in with them. *Courtesy Lisa Norton*

In the past, visitors packed suitcases full of gifts, including many luxury items that were not available in India. In recent years, however, as India produces more and more of these items, this practice has changed. However, since gift-giving is an integral part of Indian culture, most bring gifts to family and friends in India and return laden with gifts for friends and colleagues in Minnesota.

In between these visits—or in lieu of them—many Indians invite families, particularly parents, for extended stays of one to three months. Most of these visits are planned for the summer and often involve other trips and activities to show visitors around Minnesota and the United States.

Keeping in Touch

In the early years, before email and the internet, the most affordable means of communicating with family back in India was through the mail.

After the first transatlantic cable was laid in 1956 and communications satellites became operational in 1962, making international phone calls became possible—but these calls were very expensive. A single call cost four dollars a minute, and the minimum charge was twelve dollars. Not all families in India had phones at home, so "trunk calls" had to be booked either from a neighbor's phone or from dedicated phone shops (called STD booths—for "subscriber trunk dialing") run by private

That Dreaded Call

The time difference between India and the United States means that many Indians recollect a heart-stopping call that arrives in the middle of the night to inform them of the loss or serious illness of a loved one back in India.

That dreaded call usually sparks hasty preparations to leave for India—making airline reservations, informing employers, and, in the case of those who have become US citizens, getting visas. India does not allow dual citizenship, but US Indians can apply for the Overseas Citizenship of India (OCI) card, which allows them to enter India without a visa. This program, plus being able to make online travel reservations, has smoothed the way in these fraught situations.

The aerogram provided the cheapest and best way to get and share personal news, especially in early years, when many homes in India did not have telephones. Every bit of space was used to cram in as many words as possible. A few couples conducted their entire courtship by mail. When there was more to write, tissue-like paper was used to keep the weight and postage down. Mail took ten to fifteen days to reach its destination. When there was urgent news, a telegram sent via Western Union was more affordable. *Courtesy Godan Nambudiripad*

Family recipes sent by mail.
Courtesy author

business owners. The lines were often unclear and full of static, and most calls were spent shouting, "Hello" and "How are you?"

In the late 1980s, with the introduction of fiber-optic cable and competition from telephone companies, prices came down significantly. Prepaid phone cards with packaged minutes also encouraged international calling.

In recent years, with internet and email and the growth of mobile phones in India, communication has become easier, even instantaneous. Voice Over Internet Protocol (VoIP) applications such as Skype, FaceTime, or WhatsApp with video capabilities have given Indians settled in Minnesota the means to connect to loved ones in real time. Because of this instantaneous connection and the time difference between the two continents, families in India often complain that the Minnesota family members get the news before all others in India.

What's the News?: Newspapers and Magazines

Before the World Wide Web made news from all over the world easily accessible, Indians relied on newspapers and magazines to keep up with what was happening back home. In the early years, for Twin Cities residents these sources were available mainly in the Ames Library of South Asia on the Minneapolis campus of the University of Minnesota. Henry Scholberg, director and librarian from 1961 until his retirement in 1989, and assistant librarian Ella Baldwin personally knew and welcomed many Indian students who stopped at the library regularly to catch up on the news.

Many Indians also subscribed to *India Abroad* (published in New York) or the *India Tribune* (published in Chicago), which provided information on India as well as news related to Indians in other parts of the country. The *Asian American Press* (now online) and its editor Tom LaVenture still cover news related to Indians in Minnesota. Most Minnesota-Indian

Gold Mines of Information

To most Indians, a public library, where you can borrow unlimited books, is like a gold mine. For those who came before information was instantaneously available, the vast holdings of reference materials helped with many school and do-it-yourself projects. Today, despite the availability of information on the internet, many Indian parents make regular trips to the library with their kids.

Dinkytown Newsstand

From 1988 to about 1995, Indra Patel sold cigarettes and newspapers and magazines from a two-hundred-square-foot newsstand on the Fourteenth Avenue SE bridge in Dinkytown, across from the University of Minnesota. The tiny shop had a space heater but no toilet facilities, and it stocked newspapers and magazines from all over the world, including India. Among Patel's regular customers were many Indians who subscribed to popular Indian magazines such as *India Today* and *Frontline*. Patel, who came to Minnesota from Kenya, was the fifth and last owner of this stand. In 1995, when the bridge needed to be repaired, Hennepin County relocated the shop. However, declining demand for printed news eventually forced the newsstand to close in 2006.

Dinkytown Newsstand. *Courtesy Indra Patel*

organizations also produce regular newsletters to keep members informed of activities and events in the community.

In recent times, most of these stories are available online. Other sites such as Local Files provide information on services and businesses catering to Indians in Minnesota.

CELEBRATING FESTIVALS, LIFE, AND OTHER EVENTS

Indians are inherently very social and hospitable people. Inviting friends and family for meals and celebrating festivals and life events are an integral part of their upbringing. Naturally, they extend this tradition to their lives in Minnesota.

Although Indians, especially those who have lived in Minnesota for a long time or have non-Indian spouses, maintain friendships outside the Indian community, many tend to socialize with people with whom they share a common language and tradition. For those who arrived years ago, lifelong friends have become like family members, there for each other during good times and bad. This network of friends meets and socializes regularly, especially around holidays and festivals.

In the earlier years, when there were fewer Indians, get-togethers were mixed, with people from all regions of India, socializing in ways impossible back home. As the population of Indians in Minnesota has increased, gatherings have become more stratified by region or language.

Corelle Ware dishes, a brand marketed since the 1970s by Corning, were for Indians a much-coveted acquisition, a rite of passage as they settled down as immigrants in America. Besides being virtually indestructible, the compartmentalized plates and large casserole dishes were perfect for Indian buffets. One could tell when a family settled in the United States based on when the patterns on their sets were popular: Wild-flower (sixties), Blue Cornflower (seventies), Spice of Life (eighties), Just White (nineties and later).

Festivals

India is a country with diverse religions and traditions, so it is not surprising that in a single year more than thirty festivals are celebrated. Some are regionally specific,

In the early years, when restaurants and caterers were not available, hosts (mostly women) could easily spend two or more days preparing a variety of Indian dishes for their guests, usually served buffet style. *Courtesy Neena Gada*

Food is an integral part of any Indian gathering and no Indian event can be complete without serving a snack, if not an elaborate meal. Indian cuisine varies from region to region. Many who grew up in India prefer to cook and serve Indian food—often dishes from their home regions. After settling in to Minnesota, many have started cooking dishes from other regions as well as typical American fare. Though many ingenious cooks have found ways to reduce the prep time, Indian cooking can be labor intensive and involved.

Many Indians grow up with the ancient Sanskrit saying *Athithi Devo Bhava*, meaning "Guests are like gods." Guests are treated like royalty, and Indian etiquette requires hosts to repeatedly offer food and urge guests to eat—a tradition that can be confounding and perhaps even irritating to the uninitiated.

Holiday Calendar 2019

The dates for many holidays change from year to year because the Indian (Hindu) calendar is based on the phases of the moon.

JANUARY
Gyan Pachami (Jain)
Guru Govind Singh Jayanti (Sikh)
Lohri
Makar Sankranti
Pongal (Hindu)
Republic Day
Mahatma Gandhi Death Anniversary

FEBRUARY
Vasant Panchami (Hindu)
Shivaji Jayanti
Guru Ravidas Jayanti

MARCH
Maharishi Dayanand Saraswati Jayanti
Maha Shivaratri/Shivaratri (Hindu)
Holika Dahana
Holi (Hindu)
Dolyatra
Hazarat Ali's Birthday (Muslim)

APRIL
Chaitra Sukhladi
Rama Navami (Hindu)
Vaisakhi (Sikh)
Mesadi/Vaisakhadi
Ambedkar Jayanti

Mahavir Jayanti (Jain)
Passover (Jewish)
Easter (Christian)

MAY
Birthday of Ravindranath
Buddha Purnima/Vesak (Buddhist)
Jamat Ul-Vida

JUNE
Ramzan Id/Eid-ul-Fitar (Muslim)

JULY
Rath Yatra

AUGUST
India Independence Day
Bakr Id/Eid ul-Adha (Muslim)
Raksha Bandhan (Rakhi) (Hindu)
Parsi New Year
Janmashtami (Hindu)

SEPTEMBER
Ganesh Chaturthi/Vinayaka Chaturthi (Hindu)
Paryushan/Das Lakshan (Jain)
Muharram/Ashura (Muslim)
Onam

OCTOBER
Mahatma Gandhi Jayanti
Maha Saptami
Maha Ashtami
Maha Navami
Nav Ratri
Dussehra (Hindu)
Maharishi Valmiki Jayanti
Karaka Chaturthi (Karva Chauth) (Hindu)
Naraka Chaturdasi
Diwali/Deepavali (Buddhist, Hindu, Jain, Sikh)
New Year Vikram Samvant
Govardhan Puja
Bhai Duj (Hindu)

NOVEMBER
Chhat Puja (Pratihar Sashthi/Surya Sashthi)
Milad un-Nabi/Id-e-Milad (Muslim)
Guru Nanak Jayanti
Children's Day
Guru Tegh Bahadur's Martyrdom Day

DECEMBER
Hanukkah (Jewish)
Christmas (Christian)

---

some are observed all over India, and many are related to the different religions that are practiced in the country. Secular events such as Independence Day and Republic Day and birthdays of leaders such as Mahatma Gandhi are also widely commemorated.

When Indians first settled in Minnesota, opportunities to celebrate all or even a few of these festivals were rare. Diwali, the festival of lights, was one event that brought many early arrivals together. Even though Diwali is considered a Hindu/Jain festival, it has pan-Indian appeal; people gather in each other's homes for potluck dinners, regardless of religious or regional affiliations. Diwali traditionally involves lighting oil lamps and fireworks and gambling. In the United States, the oil lamps have been replaced with Christmas lights due to fire safety regulations, and not everyone plays cards. The religious part of the festival is usually performed privately with family members and sometimes close friends. In earlier years, fireworks were out of the question, but now that their use is legal in Minnesota, people stockpile them after July 4 and use them during Diwali, which usually falls during October–November. All Hindu temples in Minnesota also plan religious as well as cultural events around this festival. The Hindu Temple's Diwali celebration has grown over the years and is now held at the Minneapolis Convention Center.

In Minnesota, as the community has grown and regional and religious organizations have been established, a festival that has more significance in a specific Indian

Diwali get-together in 1968. *Courtesy Ram and Neena Gada*

The Rathayatra, or chariot festival, is celebrated annually in Minnesota by the Odisha Society. A special chariot for this festival, built and brought from India, is housed in the Hindu temple in Maple Grove. *Courtesy Hindu Mandir*

Navratri, or nine nights of celebrations before the Hindu festival of Dussehra, is celebrated differently in various parts of India. The Gujarati Samaj in Minnesota annually organizes the Garba dance to celebrate this festival. *Courtesy Gujarati Samaj*

Female energy (shakti) as symbolized in the form of a goddess is celebrated with fanfare in Bengal during the Durga Puja. The Bengali Association of Minnesota hosts this annual event. Dussera is also an important celebration in Karnataka. *Courtesy Sadanand Pathre*

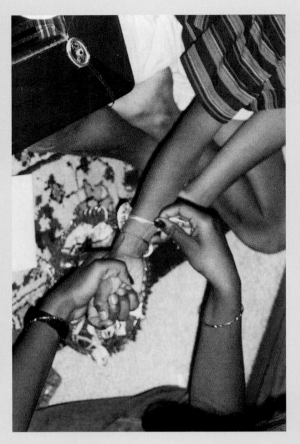

TOP Rakhee or Raksha Bandhan is a festival celebrated in individual homes mostly in North India. Sisters tie a silken or decorated cord on their brothers' wrists to symbolize their love. The rakhee tradition is so special that siblings in Minnesota separated by distance send and receive rakhees through the mail. *Courtesy author*

BOTTOM Holi is a festival held in March to welcome spring. In India it is played outdoors by throwing colored powders and water on people. Since Minnesota does not always have spring weather in March, Holi is organized indoors or moved to a later date. *Courtesy SILC*

Pongal, a four-day harvest festival, is widely celebrated in the states of Tamil Nadu, Telangana, and Andhra Pradesh in the month of January. It is also celebrated as Lohri in Punjab and as Makar Sankranti in other parts of India. On the third day of the Pongal festival, cows are decorated with garlands of flowers and taken to visit homes. *Courtesy author*

Baisakhee or Vaisakhi, a religious festival for Sikhs, marks the Punjabi new year. The Minnesota Punjabi Society organizes a cultural gathering. *Courtesy Daljit Sikka*

Onam, a harvest festival celebrated in the state of Kerala in South India, includes lighting oil lamps (above), decorating them with flowers, dancing, and serving the special Onam Sadya (feast). In Minnesota, the Malayalee Association holds a gathering with dinner and cultural performances. Traditional dishes are served on banana leaf plates (top). *Courtesy SILC and Godan Nambudiripad*

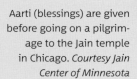

Aarti (blessings) are given before going on a pilgrimage to the Jain temple in Chicago. *Courtesy Jain Center of Minnesota*

Ganesh Chaturthi, an important Hindu celebration, is organized by the Marathi Association of Minnesota at the Hindu temple in Maple Grove. *Courtesy Sadanand Pathre*

region or religion has become the flagship event for the organization that best represents it. For instance, the Navratri festival, a nine-day event, is a major celebration in the western part of India. In Minnesota, it is celebrated in a big way by the Gujarati Samaj, a regional organization representing Gujarati-speaking members from the western state of Gujarat.

Festivals that are more religious in nature are celebrated in the appropriate place of worship. Indian Muslims, Christians, and Jews celebrate their festivals with people from other parts of the world, in their respective mosques, churches, and synagogues. Among Indian Muslims, during Ramadan, friends from other faiths are invited for iftar (breaking fast) parties.

India's Independence Day

A celebration that attracts a diverse group of Indians as well as others from the broader community marks Independence Day in mid-August. In the past, it was held as a picnic in a park, but in recent years it is celebrated at IndiaFest (previously called India Day; see page 94 for more details).

US Festivals

Besides traditional festivals, many Indian Americans celebrate Christmas socially, putting up lights, decorating Christmas trees, and exchanging gifts. Families also participate in Easter egg hunts and go trick

---

Time Out for Women

Indian women celebrate the change of seasons and other events that traditionally were held in India to bring women together to socialize. While these events may have originated in Hinduism or in a particular region, in Minnesota they are more inclusive and celebrated with a diverse group. Some of these include:

- Haldi Kumkum, a social gathering where married women exchange turmeric and vermillion.

- Varalakshmi, a South Indian tradition where married women pray for the well-being of their families. Held before the festival of Diwali.

- Karva Chauth, a North Indian festival where women fast and pray for the well-being of their husband.

For Golu, a display of dolls and figures, women gather to socialize during the nine days of Navratri, celebrated before the Dussehra festival. *Courtesy Vidya Subramani*

CLOCKWISE FROM UPPER LEFT Independence Day picnic at Snail Lake Park, Ramsey County, Minnesota, August 16, 2003. *Courtesy Roswitha Desai* • Third-generation kids celebrating Halloween and Christmas. *Courtesy Ravi Desai and Sanjukta Chaudhuri* • The Peterson-Shah family has hosted large Thanksgiving gatherings for new and old friends for more than two decades. Over the years, they have established unique traditions, with customary Thanksgiving foods as well as Indian dishes. *Courtesy Shanti Shah* • A small group of early arrivals welcomes 1968 at a New Year's Eve party. *Courtesy Ram and Neena Gada*

or treating on Halloween, and many, if not all, Indians host or attend Thanksgiving dinners (the vegetarians skip the turkey). Mother's and Father's Days are also celebrated enthusiastically.

Life Events

Indians celebrate various milestones in life from birth to death. Childhood and adolescent ceremonies include naming the baby, shaving the birth hair, feeding the first solid meal, and initiating into religious life. Ceremonies dealing with adult stages include bridal showers, weddings, baby showers, and late-in-life celebrations like sixtieth birthdays and fiftieth wedding anniversaries. Lastly are events such as death anniversaries, with homage to departed souls. As facilities for celebrating and performing these ceremonies become more readily available in Minnesota, events are increasingly being held here and not in India as in years past. Besides these traditional events, Indians also get together for housewarming and birthday ceremonies (usually the first birthday is a big affair). High school graduations are generally not celebrated in India but are widely commemorated by Indians here.

Bridal and Baby Showers—Blended Celebrations

Right from the beginning, Indian women combined Indian and US traditions when celebrating bridal and baby showers. While practices may be shifting, these parties have usually been for women only, with all guests dressing in Indian finery. The hostesses honor the bride and mother-to-be by following Indian traditions while including the American practices of games, gifts, cake, and punch.

Kamala Puram welcomes guests at a baby shower for her daughter-in-law, Askhita. *Courtesy Kamala Puram*

Weddings

Weddings are important events in India, involving many rituals and festivities, often taking place over two to three days. In the early years, not many Indian weddings were held in Minnesota. Many Indians, mostly men, would go back to India to get married after completing their education and receiving job offers and US permanent residency status. Most of these marriages were arranged by parents and family members, which was an acceptable and widespread practice in India. Often these weddings were conducted during the short span of the groom's visit to India, and the newlyweds would return to start a new life in Minnesota.

Guests at a party to welcome a new baby. *Courtesy Nayana Ramakrishnan*

A few interracial and interreligious marriages were conducted in the United States. And sometimes, when a couple could not go to India to marry due to visa or financial constraints, their weddings were also conducted here.

Most weddings during the 1960s through the 1980s were simple, makeshift affairs, arranged with help from friends and family members (if they were living in the United States or if they could come from India). Wedding decorations and food were homemade, as there were no restaurants or vendors to cater food or provide Indian wedding decorations and services. For Hindus, Jains, and Sikhs, there wasn't even a priest or a formal religious institution to perform the wedding.

Jagadish Desai and Roswitha Bullinga met in Montana but married in St. Paul in 1962. At the time, anti-miscegenation laws, abolished by the Supreme Court in 1950, were still in existence in fourteen other US states. *Courtesy Jagadish Desai*

An early Hindu (Vedic) wedding for Sekhar and Anu Ramanathan was conducted by Dr. Padmakar Dixit without any wedding decorations or Vedic ritual accouterments. *Courtesy Darlene Sheeso*

ACROSS THE TOP
Indra and Anjana Patel have tapped into the growing market for Indian weddings by renting decorations and catering food. They started in 2006 from their home's basement, but a decade later they moved the business into a warehouse. They handle twelve to fifteen weddings a year and serve as suppliers and vendors for other wedding businesses in the state. Their warehouse is well stocked with various Indian wedding essentials such as different types of mandaps (canopies), several typical Indian decorations, and liveried finery for the Baraat (processional) horses. Each year, the couple adds more decorations ordered from India. *Courtesy Indra Patel*

In 1961, Dr. Padmakar Dixit, who was born in the Brahmin or priest class and was familiar with Hindu scriptures, performed perhaps the first Vedic (Hindu) ceremony in Minnesota. However, because the State of Minnesota did not list Hinduism as a religion, he was not able to sign the marriage certificate. Later, after he successfully petitioned to have Hinduism added to the list, he was officially recognized as a Hindu priest, along with Dr. Shashikant Sane and Sesha Komanduri, who also performed weddings.

As the population of Indians in Minnesota has grown, and as second-generation Indians have started marrying, more weddings are being held in Minnesota. While weddings in India involve matching the bridal couple's horoscopes and are performed on days auspicious to them, in the United States weddings are generally held when venues are available and when convenient to all guests, such as on long weekends.

Indians tend to be inclusive, and many weddings are large, often with more than three hundred guests. US celebrations may also follow trends set in India, where weddings have become quite elaborate and lavish. Brides and their mothers make special trips to India to shop for wedding finery. These weddings have created a niche market for vendors such as wedding planners, caterers, henna artists, and decorators. As weddings are a significant revenue stream, hotel chains such as Marriott have trained their staff on Indian weddings and other celebrations to honor clients' traditions and meet their expectations.

Second-generation Indian weddings have increasingly become interracial as young Indians eschew the traditional arranged marriage and find their own mates.

However, matches are still arranged with help from friends and relatives as well as through matrimonial ads in papers such as *India Abroad* and through online services such as Shadi.com.

Many interracial marriage celebrations involve both Western (church) and Indian wedding ceremonies. Even when both the groom and the bride share Indian heritage, many couples also include, along with Indian traditions, the Western tradition of having bridesmaids and groomsmen and a reception that involves a wedding cake and speeches. They also celebrate with dancing to both Western and Indian (usually popular, Bollywood-style) music.

Wedding of Shruti Mathur and Ravi Desai with an entourage of bridesmaids and groomsmen, July 2009. *Courtesy author*

Alli and Jayesh Naithani on their wedding day in 1997. Alli combined her Indian Catholic heritage with her Minnesota upbringing by wearing the traditional white sari outfitted with a train. *Courtesy Alli Naithani*

Vishant Shah and Emily Shortridge's union in May 2000 was the first Jain wedding performed in Minnesota; it was officiated by Ram Gada. *Courtesy Ram Gada*

In the unofficial part of their wedding ceremony, Veeti and Peter, connected by a woven sash, walked seven times around the ceremonial fire, while vowing to dedicate their lives to each other. As with many weddings, the couple spoke very softly, and the priest, Sesha Kersadani, had to prompt them. The families sat nearby, showing their closeness to the ceremony and the newlyweds.

TYING THE KNOT

At the traditional henna party the day before the wedding, Veeti asked her cousin, Nidhi Kumar "Don't you want to kiss me?" Nidhi, and her sister, Nandia, instead did an impromptu Indian dance.

It's June, and the thoughts of many people turn to love and marriage.

Veeti Tandon and **Peter Sandgren** are no different. Theirs was a **Hindu wedding,** but it looked like any two happy families and two people in love.

He looked into her deep brown eyes and said quietly, "the first time we met I remember thinking that was the best date of my life."

She smiled: "It felt as if we'd known each other for years."

Peter Sandgren and Veeti Tandon were married May 27. Their families and friends came from all over, from India and Indonesia, to San Francisco and New York. Everyone was dressed to the nines, and the Interlachen Country Club in Edina sparkled.

The two were taking part in a marriage, one of the most common rites of passage.

As the bride walked down the aisle, in her mother's wedding dress, she looked at

Flower girl Sommer Schwald, Peter's 8-year-old niece, contemplates her role in the wedding. She and her mother, behind her, wore Indian dresses and hand decorations.

her waiting bridegroom, and his face beamed into sunshine.

Virtually every religion and culture registers some sort of connection of a man and a woman into a family unit. Most faiths say the union is blessed by God, and many call it a sacrament.

For society, marriage is a way of providing for the orderly transition of property, of recognizing rights and responsibilities among generations and, in general, of stabilizing life.

For Veeti and Peter marriage was a celebration of the future, and a blending of two religions and cultures.

RITES continues on B6:
Henna party marks festive occasion.

RITES OF
passage

Part three of an occasional series

Story by **Martha Sawyer Allen**
Star Tribune Staff Writer

Photos by **Stormi Greener**
Star Tribune Staff Photographer

Shashi Mangalick and Gunvent Patel at the altar during their wedding.

Staff Photo by Mike Zerby

A Hindu wedding in Minneapolis

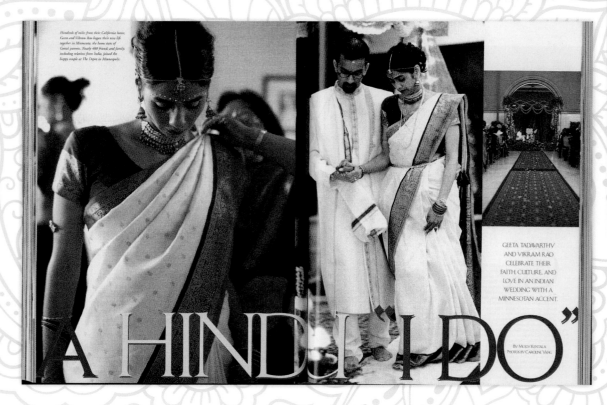

Hundreds of miles from their California home, Geeta and Vikram Rao began their new life together in Minnesota, the home state of Geeta's parents. Nearly 400 friends and family, including relatives from India, joined the happy couple at The Depot in Minneapolis.

"A HINDU I DO"

GEETA TADAVARTHV AND VIKRAM RAO CELEBRATE THEIR FAITH, CULTURE, AND LOVE IN AN INDIAN WEDDING WITH A MINNESOTAN ACCENT.

BY MOLLY KENTALA
PHOTOS BY CAROLINE VANG

Neena Gala & Ram Gada

Neena Gala married Ram Gada on April 2, 1967, in Bombay, India. As part of a marriage arranged by their parents, Ram traveled to India from his home in the United States to meet Neena for the first time. Neena, as well as both sets of parents and siblings, lived in Bombay. Indian parents are responsible for finding partners for their children who are compatible in the areas of religion, caste, status, education, and profession. After meeting just a few times, Ram and Neena decided to get married and agreed on a one-month engagement.

True to tradition, Neena wore a white sari for a pre-wedding ceremony and a red sari for the wedding. Dinner and gift parties with relatives and friends continued for a month after the wedding. Neena, who had a collection of more than 25 saris, wore a different one for each occasion during this festive period. Neena and Ram Gada currently live in New Brighton, Minnesota.

Marry in April when you can,
Joy for maiden and for man.

Indian weddings featured in the media

OPPOSITE, TOP LEFT In 1974, Shashi Manga-lick and Gunvant Patel's wedding received a lot of attention as one of the first Indian weddings to be featured prominently in the magazine section of the *Minneapolis Tribune*. Their wedding was officiated by Dr. **Usharbudh** Arya, a meditation and yoga teacher.

OPPOSITE, TOP RIGHT In 2001, the wedding of Veeti Tandon and Peter Sandgren was featured in the *Star Tribune*. The wedding was conducted by Sesha Komanduri.

OPPOSITE, BOTTOM The May 29, 2004, wedding of Geeta Tadavarthy and Vikram Rao, officiated by Sesha Komanduri, was featured in the spring/summer 2005 issue of *Minnesota Bride*. *Photos by Caroline Yang; courtesy Geeta Rao*

LEFT The Minnesota Historical Society's *Happily Ever After* exhibit in 2004 featured Ram and Neena Gada's wedding picture. *MNHS*

BELOW Deepak Nath and Sara Hlavka's lavish Las Vegas wedding was featured as a Platinum Wedding on WE TV. *Courtesy Mahendra Nath*

Worshipping and Adhering to Diverse Faiths

Indian Americans come from diverse religious backgrounds. According to the Pew Research Center (2012), among Indian Americans in the United States, 51 percent consider themselves Hindu, 18 percent Christian (Protestant, 11 percent; Catholic, five percent; other Christian, three percent), ten percent Muslim, ten percent unaffiliated, five percent Sikh, and two percent Jain. There are also a small number of Zoroastrians, Jews, and Buddhists. These statistics are also reflected among the Minnesota Indians. Many view religion as an important aspect of life and regularly participate in their own faith groups.

Hindus

Hinduism is the third-largest religion in the world, and a majority of Indian Americans in Minnesota identify as Hindu. In the early years, when there were no formal places of worship, most Hindus met in each other's homes to pray and celebrate. As the number of Hindus grew, various congregations built their own temples.

Hindus believe in one universal consciousness, Brahman, who is known to be without any form or properties that we humans can understand. The faith also supports the concept of Ishwara, a personal god (deity) to provide easy access and convenience for people who cannot relate to a formless abstract idea. Temples devoted to specific deities or philosophical thoughts have flourished in a variety of forms and shapes throughout India and are replicated here in Minnesota, particularly in the Twin Cities. Since Hinduism is a minority religion in the United States, these centers are also intended to preserve and nurture Hindu traditions and pass them on to the next generation. Like all religious institutions, they serve as community centers and bring together people of the same faith. Hindu temples are generally not places of congregation for preaching. People go there to do a darshan, a form of communion with the deity, and for personal meditation. Here in the United States, some temples host philosophical discourses on a weekly basis.

Many Indians maintain special areas in their homes for prayers and meditation. This typical Hindu puja (worship) altar is a place to light a lamp and offer daily prayers. *Courtesy Jayanti Suresh*

The Hindu Mandir, one of the largest in North America, with twenty-one mini-temples under one roof, has become a landmark and a destination site for those interested in learning about Hinduism. The temple recorded more than fifteen hundred visitors in 2018. *Photo by Morgan Sheff, courtesy MNHS*

Major Minnesota Temples

Hindu Mandir. The Hindu temple had its beginnings in individual homes. In 1979, the Hindu Society of Minnesota bought a renovated church building in Northeast Minneapolis; the purchase was financed by Shanti and P. C. Mangalick, Kumud and Shashikant Sane, and Kusum and Krishna Saxena. When the society outgrew the space, in 2006 its members built a large new temple in Maple Grove following guidelines from ancient Hindu scriptures and using traditional Hindu architectural elements. Artists were brought from India to sculpt and decorate the exterior as well as the interior structures that house many Hindu deities.

While meeting the spiritual needs of the Hindus, this temple has also become a hub for many Indian community activities and outreach. A staff of six priests is available to perform weddings and other ceremonies that honor the Hindu-prescribed stages of life, as well as cremations and death anniversaries. As a cultural center, the temple organizes events around key Hindu festivals and hosts various dance and music concerts. A school housed at the temple educates young students on Hindu

Geeta Ashram is one of the earliest Hindu organizations to be established in Minnesota. *Courtesy Kumud Kamran*

traditions and scriptures and offers a summer camp, while discourses from noted Hindu scholars and readings from the scriptures educate the adults. The temple also holds yoga and meditation sessions and, as part of its outreach program, offers temple tours, organizes blood drives, and arranges volunteers for soup kitchens.

Geeta Ashram. Geeta Ashram was started in 1972 under the inspiration of a religious leader, Swami Harihar Maharaj. At that time, member families met once a month in homes to sing bhajans (hymns), study the Bhagavad Gita, teach children prayers, and tell stories from various scriptures. In 1987, Geeta Ashram moved to a new facility in Brooklyn Park.

The building is used to hold weekly prayer and spiritual sessions, study and discuss the Gita, and practice yoga and meditation as well as hold health seminars for self-improvement and self-realization. A weekly school teaches children Indian culture and religious practices through music, dance, plays, and educational camps. Seniors in the Indian community meet there and interact with the younger generation. Geeta Ashram also provides the services of Hindu priests to perform religious ceremonies and for spiritual help during times of distress. As a cultural center, the Geeta Ashram organizes events around key Hindu festivals. Many Indian weddings, concerts, and other events such as memorials have been held there.

Other Hindu temples in Minnesota

Minnesota Hindu Dharmic Sabha Vishnu Mandir. This temple started in the early 1970s with services held in people's homes. After a few different locations, in 1995 it moved to a storefront on Lyndale Avenue in Minneapolis. Its congregation of about a hundred families is made up of first- and second-generation Hindus from Guyana and Trinidad.

Shree Satyam Mandir. This Hindu temple, currently located in a storefront in Minneapolis, was started in the 1980s, primarily to serve Guyanese youth in the Twin Cities.

BAPS Shri Swaminarayan Mandir. Members of this Hindu sect from Western India have built beautifully elaborate temples all over the world. The temple's local branch started in 1984 and meets in Brooklyn Park.

Shri Gaayatri Mandir. Founded in March 1993, this temple started as a small weekly gathering of five families in a member's basement. It eventually moved to a room in the Geeta Ashram, and then in 2004 to its own location in Northeast Minneapolis. The congregation has eighty families, all Indo-Guyanese Hindus.

Diwali (Festival of Lights) offerings at the BAPS temple.
Courtesy Ranjan Patel

Chinmaya Mission. This center is part of a global network started by Swami Chinmaya to provide Vedanta-based lessons on Hinduism to children. The Minnesota chapter was established in 1998 and is currently located in Chaska.

Minnesota Hindu Milan Mandir. Located in Farmington, this temple is home to a branch of Bharat Sevashram Sangha, an organization started in Bangladesh and locally managed by Satya Balroop since 2000. Its members are mostly immigrants from the Indo-Caribbean community and from the eastern region of India.

Sri Saibaba Mandir. This temple, located in the church that formerly housed the Hindu Mandir in Northeast Minneapolis, is a center for sharing the life and message of the saint Saibaba of Shirdi in Maharashtra, India. The service-oriented devotees are involved in many local volunteer activities. A new facility is being built in Chaska.

Hindu Samaj Temple and Cultural Center. This temple was established in 2004 to meet the needs of the growing Hindu population in Rochester.

Sri Venkateswara (Balaji) Hindu Temple. Established in 2011 in Edina by the Reddy Foundation, this temple offers religious services, conducts school classes, and provides a place for music and dance performances.

Other local Hindu organizations and their founders include:
The Art of Living Foundation
   (Usha Radhakrishnan)
Isha Institute of Inner-Sciences
   (Aravind Murali)
Krishna Sankirtan Society
   (Bheemi Reddy Kanapuram)
Minneapolis Meditation Group
   (Vivek Goel)
Sadhu Vaswani Mission
   (Tarun Karani)
Sahaja Yoga Meditation
   (Jitendra Patpatia)

Religious speakers for the community include:
Satya Balroop
Ram Gada
Anand Joglekar
Dr. Prassana Kumar
Ned Mohan
Godan Nambudiripad
Dr. Anant Rambachan
Dr. Shashikant Sane
Dr. Krishna Saxena

Indian Muslims

Indian Muslim Americans in Minnesota have and continue to worship with Muslims hailing from other parts of the world. There is no mosque or place of worship exclusively for Indian Muslims. The Anjuman-e-Asghari in Brooklyn Park, a mosque devoted to Shia Muslims, though not exclusively for Indian Americans, was established primarily by Asian Muslims who were exiled from Uganda by Idi Amin. Other subsects include the Bohra and Ismaili (founded in 1972), who also worship with other Muslims.

The Islamic Center, initially located in Dinkytown (Minneapolis), was established to serve the religious needs of Muslim international students. Later, it moved to a building in Fridley, with another branch opening in Columbia Heights in 1987. By 2018, due to a large influx of Somali Muslims, more than seventy-five mosques have been established all over Minnesota, the majority of them in the Twin Cities and a few in the St. Cloud and Rochester areas.

As with most religious institutions, all mosques serve as community centers for socializing and meeting others of Muslim faith and to impart religious lessons to youth. The Indian American Muslim Council also has a chapter in Minnesota.

Indian-Christian churches and groups in Minnesota include:
Bread of Life Full Gospel Church
Church of South India (CSI) Congregation
Global Harvest Church (Tamil Ministry)
House of Hope (Meghimai Ministries)
Indian Christian Center
Kerala Christian Congregation
Minnesota Pentecostal Assembly
St. Alphonsa Syro-Malabar Catholic Church
St. Thomas Syro-Malabar Knanaya Catholic Mission
Tamil Catholics of Minnesota (TCMN)
Telugu Christian Fellowship of Minnesota (TCFMN)
Twin Cities Tamil Catholics

Indian Christians

Like Indian Muslims, Indian Christians, both Catholic and Protestant, have assimilated with existing churches in Minnesota. However, as the number of Indian Christians has grown, several from different parts of India have gathered following their denomination's practice to hold prayer services in their respective languages and a few have even established their own churches. Many groups also meet in homes, some of them specially built to accommodate large gatherings. Indian pastors and theologians have been invited to serve in mainstream churches and to teach in seminaries. Notable among these are Reverend K. K. John, who started the Chi-Alpha Ministry Assemblies of God in 1967; the late Samuel Jones, who served in Billy Graham's ministry; and Pastor Bhushan Rao Dasari, who taught at Luther Seminary.

Sikhs

Sikhism is the world's fifth-largest religion, established in the fifteenth century, and Sikhs were the first Indian Americans to come to the United States, in the 1800s, mostly to California, where they worked as farmers and laborers. In Minnesota, most Sikhs, like other Indian Americans, work as professionals or own their own businesses. There are about 450 Sikh families living in Minnesota, mostly in the Twin Cities. Sikhs follow the teachings of Guru Nanak. A symbol of their religion is unshorn hair; Sikh men are particularly identifiable by their turbans and beards. Discrimination and

Sikh worship at the Bloomington Gurdwara: reading of the *Granth Sahib* with kirtans (hymns). *Courtesy Daljit Sikka*

violence in the United States have caused many to start shaving and stop wearing their turbans.

The Sikh Society of Minnesota, founded in 1985 under Dr. Kehar Singh and Daljit Sikka, manages the Gurdwara (Sikh place of worship) in Bloomington, where weekly services include the traditional langar, a communal meal that is served and eaten together.

Food typical of the Indian region of Punjab is served every Sunday at the Gurdwara. *Courtesy Daljit Sikka*

Jains

Jainism is one of India's ancient religions. Jains follow the teachings of its twenty-fourth teacher, Tirthankar Mahavira (527–599 BCE), and are deeply committed to three principles: ahimsa (following nonviolence), anekant (maintaining a multisided point of view), and aparigraha (limiting consumption). It is said that Mahatma Gandhi, who grew up with Jains in his home state of Gujarat, was very influenced by this philosophy, which was also practiced by his mother.

There are more than a hundred twenty Jain families in the Twin Cities. The Jain Center of Minnesota, founded by Ram Gada, Kusum Shah, and Vinod Shah, was established in October 1989. The Jain temple, its architecture representing the famous Ranakpur temple

Jain Mandir, with idols of Thirthankars (teachers). From right to left, Adinath (First), Parasnath (Twenty-third), and Mahavira Swami (Twenty-fourth). *Courtesy Ram Gada*

in Rajasthan, India, is located within the Hindu temple in Maple Grove. A school offering lessons to children ages five to fifteen is held once a month. Jains participate in monthly Satsang meetings, the annual festival of Paryushan–Das Lakshan (introspection and forgiveness), and Diwali (Mahavir Nirvan). Many Jains also attend a biennial convention hosted by Jains in North America (JAINA), held at various locations in the United States.

Zoroastrians (Parsis)

Zoroastrians follow the teachings of the Prophet Zarathustra, who was born in Persia, now Iran. Facing persecution, his followers, the Zoroastrians (known as Parsis), came to India in about the eighth century. The Parsi population in India has declined since then, with many moving to different parts of the world.

In Minnesota, about twenty-five to thirty Parsi families gather a few times a year, especially for events such as the celebration of spring equinox and Navroz (New Year's). Zoroastrians in Minnesota do not have a place of worship; occasionally a priest visits from Chicago to perform ceremonies such as Navjote (initiation to the religion). Their get-togethers usually start with Zoroastrian prayers followed by socializing and traditional Parsi food.

Indian Jews

Jews came to India around the eleventh century, and their descendants can be traced to three primary locations there: Kochi, Mumbai, and Kolkata. Most Jews have migrated to Israel and other parts of the world, and very few remain in India.

In Minnesota there are perhaps one or two Indian Jewish families; one extended family includes four siblings. Like Indian Muslims and Christians, all members of this extended family have joined mainstream congregations, worshipping and celebrating high holidays with others of their faith.

Indian Buddhists

Although Buddhism was born in India, its practitioners moved to the Far East and a large group of Buddhists in India are refugees from Tibet who, along with their leader, the Dalai Lama, are settled primarily in Dharamshala, in North India. Most Buddhists who started emigrating to Minnesota in the late 1990s from India are Tibetans.

ORGANIZING INTO CULTURAL AND SOCIAL GROUPS

People find comfort in being with those who speak their language and share their traditions. As Indians began to settle down in Minnesota, they recognized a need to organize themselves and shape their own identities, and so they formed a variety of organizations.

India is a diverse country, and its diversity is reflected in Minnesota's Indian Americans as well. The Indian constitution officially recognizes twenty-two languages and several hundred dialects; an equally substantial number of ethnic and kin groups exist, as well as numerous traditions and spiritual and religious practices. Thus, as the number of Indians in Minnesota increased in the 1970s and '80s, regional and language groups were established, as were schools and music, dance, and theater groups. With the sudden growth of the Indian population after 2000, the number of organizations has only increased.

In the early years, the first two organizations, the Indo-American Club and the India Club, included Indians from all geographical regions, languages, and religious backgrounds. Currently, there are more than fifty Indian organizations in Minnesota. Many are not only language- or faith-based but also formed due to political and social affiliations in India. For instance, organizations among the Telugu-speaking Indians in Minnesota are each associated with different regions in the former state of Andhra Pradesh. When large numbers of people from the same social kin group congregate in one city, they may unite to establish organizations such as the Agarwal Samaj or those meant to help with social causes in India, such as the Indian Organization for Rare Diseases in St. Paul.

A small percentage of Indian Americans, particularly those who came here early or have blended families, do not associate with any Indian organizations. And many second-generation Indians have wider interests and thus are involved in other organizations and activities.

All-India or Umbrella Organizations

Indian Students Association. Many educational institutions in Minnesota have informal or formal organizations for Indian students. The largest and oldest is the Indian Students Association at the University of Minnesota (ISA-UMN), which was founded as the Indo-American Club in 1946 and changed its name to the Indian Students Association (ISA) in 1986.

Members of the Indian Students Association (ISA) at the University of Minnesota include both students coming from India as well as second-generation Indians attending the university. ISA organizes Indian cultural shows, picnics, and other gatherings that bring together Indian and other students. *MNHS*

Until 1973, when India Club (now the India Association of Minnesota) was formed, the Indo-American Club was the only active organization that brought Indians together. Events hosted by the Indo-American Club included all

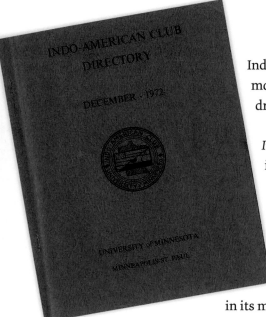

The *Indo-American Club Directory* produced in 1972 listed about six hundred Indians in the Twin Cities. *Courtesy Jagadish Desai*

Indians, not just students at the University of Minnesota. The organization's monthly Indian movie screenings on the Minneapolis campus were a big draw for Indians and a place to meet and greet newcomers to town.

India Association of Minnesota (IAM). A popular phrase from India, "Unity in Diversity," is reflected in the India Association of Minnesota's role here. IAM brings diverse Indian organizations together while also representing India to the broader society. Originally known as India Club, it has existed informally since 1970 but was incorporated as a nonprofit organization in 1973. In 1993, the name was changed to India Association of Minnesota. Popularly known as the "umbrella" organization for Indians in Minnesota, IAM includes in its mission three Cs: Charity, Culture, and Connections. Over forty-plus years of existence, it has been fulfilling its mission in these three areas.

CHARITY IAM brings the Indian community together when there is a need to help and provide support for efforts either in India or in Minnesota. IAM has collected and sent money to India in the aftermath of natural disasters such as earthquakes and floods. In October 2002, IAM brought together all of Minnesota's Indian faith groups at the state capitol for an interfaith prayer and to present a check in support of victims of the 9/11 attacks. Every summer, it organizes a golf tournament and donates the proceeds to a local or India-based charity.

CULTURE Since 1983, IAM's signature event, IndiaFest (also called India Day and Festival of India), has been showcasing Indian culture and arts, and since 1979, IAM has also been organizing and coordinating events and representing India at the Festival of Nations. In addition, it sponsors a variety of cultural opportunities with other Indian organizations as well as other events such as the Flint Hills International Children's Festival in St. Paul (partnering with the School of India for Languages and Culture).

CONNECTION As an umbrella organization, IAM represents Indians in Minnesota and connects Indians with the broader society (see pages 91–95). Through liaisons with the Council on Asian Pacific Minnesotans and events such as Connect India and Connect Asia, it ensures that the Indian community is linked with and visible to elected officials and organizations that can help the community. Connect India and IndiaFest give Indian organizations the opportunity to network with each other.

IAM also coordinates requests for speakers on India from schools and other organizations. In the past, it has sponsored special programs such as visits to nursing homes and connecting newly arrived Indian students to an Indian host family;

IAM founding members and the first board of directors were Anil Bhatnagar, Jagadish Desai, Raj Dutt, Madhukar Gupta, Robert Hoyle, Sy Mody, K. Suresh Nayak, V. Premanand, Shyamala Rajender, Bash Singh, V. C. Varadachari, and F. F. Zdenek.

> **Minnesota Asian Indian Community Directory**
>
> THE INDIA ASSOCIATION OF MINNESOTA
> (A non-profit organization)
> Since 1973
>
> **October 1998**
> Issued as part of the
> **Twenty Fifth Anniversary Celebration**
> of
> **India Association of Minnesota**

The *Minnesota Asian Indian Directory* was compiled by board members Sarat Mahapatra and Vasant Sukatme in 1998 to commemorate the India Association of Minnesota's twenty-fifth anniversary. The directory serves as a time capsule, listing Indians and their organizations before the technology boom brought hundreds more to Minnesota. *Courtesy author*

Connect India, originally called IAM Dinner, has grown over the years. The event brings together the Indian community and its nonprofit organizations to network with prominent Minnesota leaders and honors IAM achievement awardees for excellence in community service. *Courtesy IAM and SILC*

As large numbers of Indian American families put down roots in the Fargo-Moorhead area, the Indo-American Association of the Great Plains (IAAGP) was formed in 2002 to promote awareness of Indian culture, pass traditions to the next generation, and organize community programs and celebrations.

it helped establish the Asian Indian Women's Association (AIWA) and the Indian seniors group called 55+, and organized oral history projects and the *Beyond Bollywood* exhibit with the Minnesota Historical Society. Other events, such as nonviolence days and peace marches, bring a wide group of people together to reinforce Mahatma Gandhi's message of nonviolence and to march in solidarity against racial discrimination.

Regional, State-Based, or Language Organizations

India's diversity is reflected in the large spectrum of organizations formed in Minnesota that are based on geographical regions and languages of India. These organizations plan gatherings around festivals and events that are significant in their regions in India. Many also have affiliated organizations at the national level. As their membership has grown, these regional groups have invited artists from India and arranged concerts, plays, and films in their respective languages.

Arts Organizations

Performing arts organizations, artists, and schools are preserving and passing on the ancient traditions of Indian dance and music—both classical and modern genres. Many local singers and musicians have been contributing to the world music and dance scene in Minnesota through their performances and collaborations. Several offer classes and are helping their students, particularly second-generation Indians, stay connected with their Indian heritage. Two theaters founded by Indian Americans, while not focused solely on Indian drama, have produced plays with Indian themes.

Music

Indian Music Society of Minnesota (IMSOM). Formed in 1980, IMSOM has been successful in bringing many internationally known musicians and singers from India to the Twin Cities. Their events expose Indians as well as members of the broader community to both genres of classical Indian music: the styles of North India (Hindustani) and South India (Carnatic). IMSOM also cosponsors concerts and events by local artists and art-based organizations.

Indian Music Society of Minnesota logo.
Courtesy A. Pavan

IMSOM supports the annual community music event Aradhana, held to celebrate the birth of Saint Tyagaraja, a man revered for his role in developing the Carnatic musical tradition. A talented pool of local singers and musicians gather to perform his compositions. *Courtesy Vijay Ramanathan*

Trevor Barrett, one of the recipients of the Dr. J. Premanand Scholarship, holds the dedication plaque for the Dr. V. Premanand Theatre and Concert Hall. *Courtesy Normandale Community College Foundation*

In early years, small informal musical gatherings were held in people's homes. As these events grew, they moved to various auditoriums around the Twin Cities and began attracting diverse audiences. Many concerts are held at the Dr. V. Premanand Theatre and Concert Hall at Normandale Community College in Bloomington, built to honor the memory of one of IMSOM's founding members. In recent years, smaller gatherings are being revived, reflecting the traditional Indian style of performing classical music.

Alternate or Popular Music. A genre from Indian films popularly known as Bollywood music has always appealed enormously to a wide and diverse group of Indians. At social gatherings in Indian homes, singing Indian film songs is a popular form of entertainment. In recent years, with the run-away success of *Slumdog Millionaire*, Bollywood music has also been attracting an international audience.

Vijay Ramanathan, one of the first to start a band in this genre, says, "Around 1995 or so, a few of us individuals interested in singing film songs started performing at local organization events." In recent years, as the number of temporary technical workers from India has risen, the pool of talent and interest has increased and several bands and groups have performed at various local events such as IndiaFest. Many of these musicians are also experimenting with music from other countries, creating a vibrant fusion-music scene in Minnesota.

InFusion made their debut at IndiaFest. This nine-member Indian band plays contemporary fusion rock including Bollywood-style musical numbers. *Courtesy IAM*

Dr. Pooja Goswami Pavan often performs and collaborates with her husband, Dr. A. Pavan, who plays the tabla, the North Indian percussion instrument.

Dr. Pooja Goswami Pavan is a multifaceted performer, composer, teacher, and scholar of Hindustani (North Indian classical) vocal music. A recipient of multiple prestigious National Scholarships in India as well as the McKnight Fellowship for Musicians, Pavan has taught several courses in Indian music and culture at the University of Minnesota and Macalester College since moving to Minnesota in 2006.

A versatile performer, she sings several classical as well as folk-inspired forms of North Indian music. Her recordings feature several original Sufi, ghazal, and bhajan compositions. She has collaborated with Ananya Dance Theatre, Katha Dance Theatre, Pangea World Theater, and Cedar Cultural Center in many original works and performances.

Nirmala Rajasekar is one of the world's foremost exponents of the Carnatic—South Indian classical—musical style. Rajasekar travels globally performing as a Saraswati veena player and vocalist, collaborating across disciplines and genres, and recording internationally acclaimed albums. As artistic director of the Naadha Rasa (Essence of Tone) Center for Music, she educates students who perform throughout the United States and India. A recipient of the Bush Fellowship, the McKnight Fellowship, and the Rotary Club's Vocational Excellence Award, Nirmala serves on the board of directors of the American Composers Forum.

Nirmala Rajasekar

Dance

Reflecting India's diversity, several groups in Minnesota teach and perform various classical Indian dance styles.

From humble beginnings at the School of India for Languages and Culture (SILC) in the 1980s, Katha Dance Theatre and Ragamala Dance Company, two prominent local Indian dance groups, have now moved on to international stages. In recent years, several companies have formed to teach and perform other classical dance styles as well as the popular modern dance style called Bollywood dance. These schools are helping Indians in Minnesota preserve their culture and pass it along to the next generation. Through outreach programs, many of them are also giving back to the community at large and helping enrich Minnesota culturally and socially.

Katha Dance Theater (KDT). Founded in 1987 by Rita Mustaphi, KDT creates, performs and educates through the arts of dance, music, poetry, and storytelling. KDT is dedicated to making Kathak dance—the classical style of North India—accessible, inclusive, and relevant. It enhances the community by bridging diverse cultures and audiences to contribute to life's infinite artistic expressions.

Ragamala Dance Company was founded by Ranee Ramaswamy in 1992. Along with daughters Aparna and Ashwini, the company has been creating collaborative performances that showcase Indian spirituality based on the South Indian classical dance form, Bharatanatyam. Combining this ancient dance with contemporary aesthetics, the company performs not only in Minnesota but for audiences at prestigious venues all over the world. Ranee Ramaswamy was appointed by President Barack Obama to the National Council on the Arts, which advises the chair of the National Endowment for the Arts.

Rita Mustaphi

Other dance companies:
Angika Dance Academy (2010), founded by Sujatha Akurati
Aniccha Arts (2004), founded by Pramila Vasudevan
Flute 'n Feather Dance Company, founded by Priya Murali
Kala Vandanam Dance Company, founded by Suchitra Sairam
Kuchipudi Dance Academy, founded by Purnima Dasari
Natyakala Dance Academy (2009), founded by Sona Nair Menon
Nritya Kalakshetra Dance Academy, founded by Sivanuja Balaji
Nrityalaya Dance Academy (1992), founded by Padmaja Dharnipragada

Ranee Ramaswamy

Ananya Chatterjea

Ananya Dance Theatre. Founded in 2004 by Ananya Chatterjea, professor of dance at the University of Minnesota, this company brings together women of color to perform contemporary compositions influenced by the "group theater of Kolkata." Their productions combine dance with activism; while engaging audiences with powerful movements, they advocate themes of social justice.

R. G. K. Modern Indian Dance Company. Founded in 2004 by Renu Kumar, this company presents dance dramas that combine traditional Indian dance with modern movements—a style known as Bollywood dancing. Often these dance dramas revolve around a single theme with several expressions of that theme. Proceeds from many productions are donated to local causes.

Renu Kumar   Divya Maiya

South Asian Arts and Theater House (SAATH), formerly Bollywood Dance Scene. Founded in 2012 by Divya Maiya, Jinal Vakil, and Rashi Mangalick, this company promotes cultural understanding and social justice issues through dance/music and community involvement, presenting two to four community-based performances monthly. It collaborates with and contributes to several local nonprofits aligned with its mission. It performed the first live Bollywood dance drama at the Minnesota Fringe Festival.

Theater

Two groups founded by Indian Americans contribute to Minnesota's thriving theater scene.

Pangea World Theater. Founded in 1995 by Dipankar Mukherjee and Meena Natarajan, Pangea World Theater produces and presents plays that are inclusive of all cultures and voices. It works with a wide variety of underrepresented people, including artists of color, indigenous artists, women, and members of the LGBTQ+ community.

The short-lived group **Abhinay** (1995-97) was founded by Dipankar Mukherjee and Pramod Mathur to expose Indian American youth to theater arts.

Dipankar Mukherjee   Meena Natarajan

Dreamland Arts. Zaraawar Mistry and his wife, Leslye Orr, created this theater space in 2006 to showcase various performing artists and productions in an intimate setting. Mistry has highlighted his background through productions that involve children's stories from India and narratives from growing up as a Zoroastrian in India.

Zaraawar Mistry

Pangea Theater's *5 Weeks* brought to stage the traumatic effects of the 1947 partition between India and Pakistan. *Courtesy Pangea Theater*

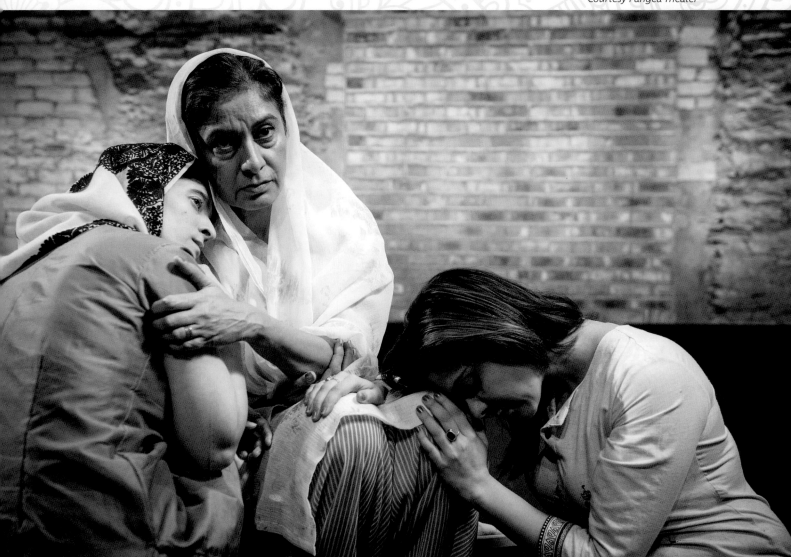

For forty years, the School of India for Languages and Culture has been one of the very few schools teaching Indian culture in a non-religious setting. *Courtesy Gundu Rao and Raj Menon*

Schools

As Indian immigrants started settling down in Minnesota, parents wanted their children to learn about and have pride in their Indian heritage. To that end, many schools have been established, primarily in the Twin Cities. While most are faith based, the longest running—School of India for Languages and Culture (SILC)—has always been secular and remains unique even among other Indian schools across the United States.

Depending on each school's mission, a variety of classes are generally held on weekends. A few schools offer summer camps as well.

The *School of India for Languages and Culture (SILC)* was established in 1979. Previously known as Bharat School, it was reorganized as a nonprofit organization to teach children Indian languages and culture in a secular environment inclusive of all Indian religions and regions. This weekend school offers classes in Indian languages, geography, history, and culture and electives such as yoga, music, and cooking. A preschool introduces children (ages three to five) to their Indian heritage. Held once a month, it encourages younger kids, particularly siblings, to attend SILC and become regular students later.

Besides attending weekly classes, students also participate in cultural programs at local events including Festival of Nations, IndiaFest, and Flint Hills International Children's Festival. Many of SILC's graduates attribute their comfort with their Indian heritage to time spent in the school's programs.

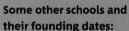

The Bharat School was founded by Dr. K. P. S. Menon. SILC founding/executive members were Neena Gada, Usha Kumar, Preeti Mathur, Rita Mustaphi, Prabha Nair, Rijuta Pathre, and Shanti Shah.

Some other schools and their founding dates:
BAPS Swaminaryan (1984)
Jain Pathshala (1989)
Chinmaya Balavihar School (2002)
Minnesota Tamil Sangam (MNTS) School (2008)
Hindu American Temple School (HATS) (2009)
Gayatrei (Geeta Ashram) (2010)
Sri Venkateswara Temple School (2011)
Twin Cities Tamil Padasalai (2013)

"SILC gave me an opportunity to learn and express my culture. It helped me define and develop my identity and, most importantly, to interact with others who shared similar experiences of growing up in a bicultural environment."
Neelima Babu, former SILC student

Wellness and Social Services Organizations

The growth of the Indian population in Minnesota has meant changes in some of the characteristics that initially defined the community. Today, not every Indian here is highly educated or a professional, and not all are wealthy, young, or in the best of health.

Unfortunately, the social construct that Indians are a "model minority" masks existing problems as well as availability of and access to funding and resources. As with all communities, there are incidents of domestic violence and senior abuse as well as mental and health problems in the Indian community. And, as with many communities, these incidents and problems are often viewed as stigmas and hence not shared or talked about openly. Many suffer in silence out of fear of "losing face or bringing shame to the family." Thus, any help to resolve or treat these issues needs to be culturally sensitive as well.

In 1995, the short-lived Asian Indian Women's Association (AIWA) initiated awareness for creating social services organizations in the Indian community. *Courtesy Neena Gada*

Two organizations in the Indian community have begun to address these challenges. While their work overlaps in some areas, SEWA–Asian Indian Family Wellness (*sewa* means "service") focuses on immediate and existing needs and AshaUSA (*asha* means "hope") seeks to help prevent these challenges. Both offer culturally sensitive programs for women and seniors.

> "As the Indian community is growing, so are the challenges. AshaUSA and SEWA-AIFW can barely scratch the surface in meeting these challenges. The Indian community needs to step up to ensure that these organizations have the necessary resources to meet the growing challenges in the community."
> Kamala Puram, founder, AshaUSA

SEWA–Asian Indian Family Wellness (SEWA-AIFW) was founded in 2004 by Raj Chaudhary to deal with challenges arising from growth in the Indian community. The organization offers an all-hours crisis hotline, protection and preventive services for women in abusive relationships, and health education and care for women, homebound seniors, and underserved individuals.

AshaUSA was founded in 2014 by Kamala Puram to promote health and harmony in the South Asian community living in Minnesota. The organization offers culturally specific programs to meet the community's needs, engages in research to understand the challenges community members face, and educates professionals such as medical practitioners, teachers, lawyers, and law enforcement to increase awareness of South Asian culture.

Entertainment

When it comes to media entertainment, few radio or TV shows dedicated to Indian programming have launched in Minnesota. However, Indian movies and programs brought into the home through streaming or satellite TV and screened in movie houses continue to provide entertainment to many Indians in Minnesota.

Radio
Radio Sangam is the longest-running Indian radio program, airing since 1990. It is broadcast every Monday from 8 to 10 PM on KFAI Fresh Air, a community radio station. Started by Mukhtar Thakur and Sarjit Bains and also cohosted by Shashi Gupta,

the program plays popular Indian music with the catchy tag, "all the hits this side of Bombay on this side of town."

Sounds of India was the first Indian radio program in Minnesota, broadcast on KUXL (Golden Valley) from September 1975 to May 1976. It featured popular Indian music as well as topics of interest to the Indian community. The show was hosted by Raj Chaudhary, Suraksha Gulati, and M. J. Abhisekhar.

Shashi Gupta, *Radio Sangam*

Sarjit Bains, one of the hosts of *Radio Sangam*, which airs on KFAI Community Radio. *Courtesy SILC*

TV Programs

ChaiCity aired weekly on Twin Cities Public Television (TPT, Channel 17) and a few community cable channels from 2001 through 2007. Founded by Pramod Mathur, Manila Mathur, and Simone Ahuja, it served the South Asian community with programs that highlighted local Indian events, music, dance, and interviews with visiting artists from India.

Geetmala and *Diversity in Focus*, two programs geared primarily to the Indian community in Minnesota, were started by Mukhtar Thakur and produced and managed by a host of volunteers. St. Paul Neighborhood Network (SPNN) provided equipment, studio and editing space, and production training to the volunteers, and the shows were broadcast on Twin Cities Public Television. Both programs ceased in 2014.

Geetmala aired on St. Paul Neighborhood Network. *Courtesy SILC*

Indo-American Club Newsletter advertisement for a movie screening in the 1970s. *MNHS*

Movies

India is the largest producer of feature films in the world, and Hindi films, often referred to as Bollywood films, have been extremely popular since the early days of Indian cinema. Indian films were the main source of entertainment in the Indian community in the late 1960s and early 1970s. Movies were screened at the Bell Museum, on the University of Minnesota's east bank campus. Later, the Indo-American Club (now the Indian Students Association) regularly screened Bollywood blockbusters at Willey Hall on the west bank. These movies were rented from Indian movie distributors; organizers dashed to the airport to pick up and send back the reels. The screenings were early places for Indians to meet one another and where newcomers were introduced to others.

In the 1980s, when videocassette recorders (VCRs) and videos became popular, the movie screenings were replaced by video rental shops. Asia Imports Groceries and Intercontinental Video (both now closed) and others did brisk business renting Indian movies. Since the VCR format differed between the United States and India, a few movie fans even owned equipment that ran videos in Indian format so they could bring videos back from their trips to India.

By the early 2000s, satellite dish programs became available, and many Indians subscribed to channels such as Zee TV and TV Asia that broadcast not only Bollywood films and Hindi programming but news and films in many other regional languages. In recent years, theaters in Brooklyn Park and Eden Prairie have started screening Indian movies at the same time as they are released in India. Throughout the world the audiences for these movies have grown so large that film producers in India are making movies set in the United States and United Kingdom using non-resident Indians (NRIs) as protagonists.

Streaming digital services such as Netflix and Amazon also offer many Indian film titles. In 2019, Eros International, an Indian film distributor, got into the digital streaming business, offering subscriptions and producing shows specially geared toward Indian families in the United States.

"We really looked forward to these monthly movies. There were a few of us newly married couples, and we would get all dressed up in Indian clothes and jewelry to go to these movies."
Kokila Mody, an early arrival

Om Puri, who has a PhD in genetics, ran Intercontinental Video in the Cedar-Riverside neighborhood for thirty-five years. His store had a large collection of foreign films, including old Bollywood movies. In 2017, affected by technology changes (from video to DVD to cable to internet streaming services), he had to close shop.

Sports

Many Indians, particularly of the second generation, are actively involved in sports such as baseball, soccer, football, tennis, and volleyball. But for a significant number of Indians, especially those who grew up in India, nothing can beat their passion for cricket.

Indians have played a significant role in developing cricket in Minnesota. In 1986, the Continental Cricket

Courtesy author

Courtesy Ram Gada

Courtesy Godan Nambudiripad

Courtesy Vaman Pai

Minnesota Indian Cricket
Team. *MNHS*

Club was organized by Sandeep Hirekerur and students from the University of Minnesota. This team was later folded into the Minnesota Cricket Association (MCA); its members, including several Indians, compete with teams from other states.

The MCA, established in 1976, originally had mostly players from the Caribbean and played its games in the summer at Bryn Mawr Meadows in Minneapolis. Today twenty-nine teams meet for games played in six different venues. The association now includes women and youth teams and has introduced a variety of playing formats.

In 1988, a Minnesota team played a match with top-ranking Indian cricketers Sunil Gavaskar, G. R. Viswanath, Mohammad Azharuddin, Anshuman Gaekwad, and Maninder Singh.

Inviting Artists and Dignitaries from India

Over the years, Minnesota Indians have maintained their cultural links by inviting artists from India for performances as well as dignitaries such as Indian ambassadors and consulate staff for meet-and-greet events. Proximity to Chicago, with its large Indian American population, has inspired many artists and dignitaries to extend their tours to include the Twin Cities.

Organizations such as the Indian Music Society of Minnesota, Ragamala Dance Company, and Katha Dance Theatre have for many years been inviting professional artists of international repute. Audiences in Minnesota have had better opportunities to attend performances of world-class artists such as Ravi Shankar and Zakir Hussain and dancers such as Alarmél Valli and Birju Maharaj than their counterparts in India. These performances have also helped educate and expose other Minnesotans to India's rich and diverse culture.

Birju Maharaj, a Kathak dancer of international repute, has come to Minnesota more than once to perform and teach students of Katha Dance Theatre. *Courtesy Rita Mustaphi*

Alarmél Valli (center), the foremost exponent of the Pandanallur style of Bharatanatyam dance, with senior students and Ranee Ramaswamy and Aparna Ramaswamy of the Ragamala Dance Company in Minnesota. *Photo by Tim Koering*

As Minnesota's Indian population has grown, concerts and events featuring popular Indian film stars and singers from India have become economically feasible. These large concerts—similar to pop concerts—are held in venues like the Minneapolis Convention Center. *Courtesy author*

Ambassador T. N. Kaul (center) on a 1975 visit to the Twin Cities, with banker Dharani Narayan (left) and Jagadish Desai (right). *Courtesy Jagadish Desai*

Former Indian president Abdul Kalam at a banquet organized by the India Association of Minnesota and the Venkateswara Temple, May 23, 2013. *Courtesy IAM*

Indian Ambassador Abid Hussain (right) with Ram and Neena Gada during his March 16, 1992, visit to Minnesota. *Courtesy Ram and Neena Gada*

Nobel Peace Prize winner Kailash Satyarthi and wife Sumedha attend a fund-raiser at Dr. S. K. and Kalpana Dash's home in 2018. Kailash also lectured at the Hindu temple during his visit. *Courtesy IAM*

Contributing to Causes in India

Many Minnesota Indians consciously give back to India through organizations they have started or through established nonprofits. Additionally, many Indians in Minnesota regularly send money to family in India and support their own personal causes there. During national crises such as earthquakes and floods, Indians (through the Indian Association of India and related regional organizations) have set up fund-raisers to send money for relief.

One of the first Indian-led fund-raisers in Minnesota was a concert in 1973 by the Indian film singer Talat Mahmood. Proceeds were donated for drought relief in India. Earlier, in 1972, the Indo-American Club organized a concert by film actress Asha Parekh and dancer Gopi Krishna.

The NRI Homecoming, a movement that coincided with economic liberalization in India in 1991, encouraged many Indians settled in the United States and other countries to start nongovernmental organizations (NGOs) to support various causes in India. *NRI Homecoming* refers to this international effort by non-resident Indians (NRIs), people of Indian origin who did not live in India but who collectively wanted to give back to their birth country. The movement included several Minnesotans.

In 2001 Minnesota Indians collected $275,000 for the Gujarat earthquake fund, which helped rebuild the entire village of Vijaypar in Kutch as well as support a medical mobile van to treat women with health issues at Bhojay, Kutch. In later years, Minnesota Indians also collected and sent funds to help victims of the 2004 tsunami and the 2018 floods in Kerala.

Professor Ram Dayal Munda, the only member of the Munda Indian tribe to come to the United States in the 1970s, taught at the University of Minnesota. He used his education and involvement with the UN Working Group on Indigenous Populations to uplift and help his tribe. *Minnesota Daily*

Where the Brahmaputra Meets the Mississippi, a fund-raiser bringing two cultures together, has been held annually since 2004. Proceeds from the show support teacher training workshops as well as science and math camps in Assam schools. *Courtesy Geeti Das*

A dilapidated school in Alwar, Rajasthan, was transformed and upgraded by Sehgal Foundation with support from Minnesota donors who were inspired to give back to their country of origin. A second Minnesota-supported school in Medchal District, Telangana, will be completed in 2019. *Courtesy Sehgal Foundation*

A few philanthropic initiatives in India supported by Minnesota Indians are:

Aavishkaar Nari Gunjan, a school to teach underprivileged girls science and math (Sandhya Gupta)

Minnesota chapter of Asha, an organization for educating underprivileged children

Begunahi Foundation, educates and empowers underprivileged women (Riaz Aziz and Mary DeLana Duffy-Aziz)

Children's Health Awareness Nurturing Care and Education (CHANCE), helps underprivileged children in India with basic education, health, and development needs (Shambhu Nath)

Durgadutt Family Foundation, Binapani School for Blind-Deaf Girls (Jugal Agarwal)

Eye Hospital in Agra (P. C. Mangalick Charitable Fund)

Indian Organization for Rare Diseases (Dr. Ramaiah Muthyala)

Indika Alliance, an organization to uplift girls and women working as maids (Denise D'Rozario, cofounder)

Minnesota Millennium Initiative, provides food to toddlers (Dr. Bharat Parekh)

People Using Self Help to Push Ahead (PUSHPA), empowers people at the grassroots level in rural South India (Gummadi Franklin and Shirley Franklin)

Ramkrishnan Family Trust, helps implement water-harvesting projects in famine-stricken areas in India

Reddy Foundation (Dr. Jyothsna Reddy and Madhu Reddy)

SwaraVedika, teenage singers raising funds to help underprivileged students in India and the United States (Kamalakar Kanjam)

Minnesota chapter of Vibha USA, an organization to uplift children (Mihir Jawale and K. Nambudiripad)

VidyaGyan, provides education and humanitarian services (Dr. Vijendra Agarwal and Dr. Indu Agarwal)

Seshaaiyar Ramakrishnan featured in *Economic Times—Madras Plus. Courtesy Nayana Ramakrishnan*

Seshaaiyar Ramakrishnan, who came to Minnesota from Chennai in 1969 to study at the University of Minnesota and ran a successful software business, began promoting harvesting rainwater to deal with acute water shortages in his birth city of Chennai. His idea took root there and was widely implemented, especially after the state's chief minister, Jayaram Jayalalithaa, endorsed it. Through his organization, Akash Ganga, he worked with other states in India as well. He has also been an ardent proponent of renewable energy and initiated a solar-energy installation at the Hindu temple in Maple Grove.

Dr. S. K. Dash through the Dr. Dash Foundation has made charitable donations to many Indian organizations and causes in the state of Odisha, India:

Fakir Mohan University
Indian Institute of Technology, Bhubaneswar
Kalinga Hospital Foundation, Bhubaneswar
Odisha Dance Academy
Regional Blood Bank, Bhubaneswar
SitaKantha PolyTech School
Utkal Samilani
several orphanages and high schools

5 *Dealing with Discrimination, Adversity, and Loss*

As with every community, Indian Americans have faced a variety of adversities and losses and have dealt with discrimination, racism, and prejudice.

DEALING WITH DISCRIMINATION

Despite success in school and employment, and although the majority of Indian Americans are educated and fluent in English, many have stories to tell about facing various forms of prejudice, racism, and discrimination.

Discrimination has ranged from overt hostility during and after national crises like the Iran hostage crisis in 1979–81 and 9/11 to more subtle forms, such as being overlooked for promotion, stereotyped as illiterate, or treated as an employee rather than a supervisor.

During the Iran hostage crisis, many Indians with the last name Shah were picked out from phone books and harassed with late-night calls. Sikh men who wore turbans were mistaken for Muslims and called "Ayatollah." Many Indian Minnesotans felt fearful after the 2017 presidential inauguration when anti-immigrant attackers committed acts of violence and harassment against Indian Americans in other parts of the country.

Indians who settled in the 1960s recalled instances of discrimination, such as when an Indian student could not rent an apartment near the University of Minnesota and the caretaker confessed it was against the owner's policy to rent to a person of color. Or how the private, gated community of North Oaks would not allow people of color—Blacks, Asians, and even Jews—to build homes. This tale seems unbelievable today, given that more than thirty Indian American families live there now.

In 1973, Shyamala Rajender, an assistant professor of chemistry at the University of Minnesota, filed a class action lawsuit when she was denied tenure. She won, and the landmark case paved the way for other women professors. Other Indian women have faced similar discrimination.

Given the gender bias that existed at that time, Jayseetha Premanand, who received a PhD in theoretical physics in 1962, was dissuaded from seeking a research position at the University of Minnesota. Fortunately, she went on to a long career teaching mathematics at Normandale Community College, where she later established scholarships and built an auditorium dedicated to the memory of her late husband.

In 2006, the Hindu temple in Maple Grove was vandalized by two young men. Besides damaging the property, they also destroyed deities that were to be consecrated. When they were apprehended, the Hindu community asked the judge not to sentence the young men to jail but to let them perform community service, thereby demonstrating the Hindu principles of tolerance and forgiveness. The deities were buried on the temple grounds, where a garden dedicated to peace was planted.

On March 4, 2017, the India Association of Minnesota organized a peace march in Eden Prairie in memory of Srinivas Kuchibhotla, who was fatally shot in Kansas, to show solidarity against hate and violence. Although in Minnesota Indians have not faced overt violence like the Dotbuster attacks in New Jersey or the 2012 killing of Sikhs in Wisconsin, the community has been vigilant. Members have gotten involved in social and political activism to combat these issues and to make sure their voices are heard. Many older citizens who remember the expulsion of Indians in East Africa and the Japanese internment camps in the United States have been instrumental in involving Indian Americans in civic and political activities.

As the Indian population in Minnesota continues to grow and as awareness of India and Indians increases through encounters in workplaces, media, and neighborhoods, Indians are being recognized for their technical aptitude, business acumen, service, and many contributions to Minnesota.

Dealing with and Overcoming Adversities

As with any other community, Indian Americans have faced various adversities. Coping with disabled children or caring for a family member with serious or long-term debilitating illnesses requires a can-do mindset, strong faith, and tremendous fortitude. A few community members shared their stories—profiles in courage.

When *Jaya and Rathna Somasundaram*'s granddaughter, *Nicole Singaram*, was born six weeks early, no one expected her to live. But she defied the odds and is now in her twenties. Her premature birth led to many disabilities, including deafness. To communicate with her and ensure she is included in all conversations and activities, her entire family—parents, grandparents, aunts, and cousins—has learned sign language. In recent years, Nicole has also started losing her vision. Her mother, Shanthi, who grew up in the Twin Cities and has given up her own career as a chemical engineer to help Nicole succeed, says, "As children, my sisters and I had to learn to integrate American and Indian cultures. Now my daughter not only is growing up Indian American; she has the added complexity of also belonging to the deaf culture. Nicole wrote a paper in school about integrating her three cultures!"

Rijuta and Sadanand Pathre's second daughter, *Minakshi (Minu)*, was born with cerebral palsy, quadriplegia, and severe intellectual impairments. In the pre-internet era, her family learned all they could by scrounging through books and medical literature on her condition.

Minu with her parents, Rijuta and Sadanand Pathre. *Courtesy Sadanand Pathre*

Minakshi's mother, Rijuta, connected with Partners in Policymaking, a leadership training program provided by the Minnesota Governor's Council on Developmental Disabilities. As a parent of a child with disabilities, she also got involved with various advocacy groups, state government advisory councils, boards, and task forces to make recommendations to implement and improve policies on special education and to help introduce a system to disseminate this information. She was invited to serve on the Minnesota State Quality Council, which worked to change the laws and policies that were detrimental to people with disability and fought for their rights to dignity and respect.

Determined not to institutionalize their daughter and despite their own health issues, Rijuta and Sadanand have looked for ways to take care of Minu at home, which they have successfully done for forty years and counting.

Dr. Paul Singh was only fifty-four when he was diagnosed with Parkinson's disease in 1984. A successful pediatrician, he continued to work and help with his young patients for another decade before retiring from his practice. A man of faith, he did not cut his hair and continued to wear the turban as prescribed by the Sikh religion.

Dr. Singh and his wife, Bash, moved to Minnesota from Tennessee in 1972 and the next year were the first Indian family to live in the gated community of North Oaks. They built a house there in 1989, but when his illness progressed, they moved again, to a handicap-accessible townhouse in the same neighborhood, in 2003.

The couple strongly believed in assimilating outside the community and staying involved in various activities. With the help of a team of personal attendants, they continued to attend social events and travel. Dr. Paul Singh passed away in 2012, after twenty-eight years of living with Parkinson's.

Harshad (Hap) Bhatt came to Minnesota in 1977, starting his career at Litton Microwave and eventually becoming a senior leader at Control Data Corporation. He was a dedicated member of the Indian community, holding leadership roles in organizations such as the School of India for Languages and Culture and the Gujarati Samaj.

Like many Indians of his era, he overcame adversities that affected his career and ability to support his family. Unfortunately, he met his ultimate hardship of early-onset Alzheimer's in his early sixties. Dementia and other debilitating mental conditions were new to the Indian immigrant community at that time. When Harshad

Harshad Bhatt and his wife, Rekha, at the seaport in Mumbai on the eve of his departure to the United States. *Courtesy Rekha Bhatt*

started showing signs of confusion, no one suspected anything was amiss, as he had a penchant for joking.

As his disease progressed, it became challenging for the family to get the support they needed in Minnesota. Harshad and his wife, Rekha, who was battling cancer, moved to Chicago, where he had close friends from his early years in the United States. When it was difficult to care for him at home because of Rekha's illness, he was moved to an assisted-living facility, where, ironically, he thought he was volunteering and would visit and help with other residents. He passed away in 2011.

Apart from illnesses and physical disabilities, some members of the community have also had to deal with mental disabilities, which, as in the broader society, are often taboo subjects and not openly discussed. Organizations such as SEWA-AIFW and AshaUSA (see page 68) and psychologists provide culturally sensitive help.

SEWA-AIFW and AshaUSA are also collaborating with Anjuli Mishra Cameron, research director for the Council on Asian Pacific Minnesotans and a second-generation Indian, to influence legislators to fund culturally sensitive programs to end domestic violence.

Asha Sharma, a second-generation Indian, runs Disability Partners, PLLC, a firm that helps clients navigate the Social Security disability program by filing disability claims with the Social Security Administration and representing clients at disability hearings. Psychologists such as Enakshi Choudhuri, Asha Mukherjee, and Zehra Ansari volunteer their time educating the community at large about mental health and working directly with people who need help.

Dealing with Losses

When Indians were first settling in Minnesota, community members were young and deaths were few and far between. In recent years, as the early settlers and the parents who came to live with their children are aging, Indians have had to deal with a lot more losses.

In the early years, Muslims and Christians could rely on their mosques and churches for help with funerals, but for Hindus, Jains, and Sikhs, there were no priests or facilities to perform the last rites. Dr. Padmakar Dixit, who grew up as a Brahmin (priest class) and knew the rituals, was often called upon to perform the last rites for Hindu funerals. Today, memorials and death anniversaries are performed in religious institutions as prescribed by each faith.

Indians are a close-knit group, and when tragedies and losses occur, the entire community comes together to provide support. This sense of unity certainly was true in the early years, but even today, close friends rally to comfort the bereaved, help with funeral arrangements, and bring meals. While suicides are not common in the Indian community, they have occurred and often are not discussed, as there is a stigma surrounding them.

Over the years, Minnesota funeral homes have become familiar with Indian funerals and have made efforts to accommodate the different rituals practiced among Indians. Since Indian funerals tend to draw larger-than-normal numbers of visitors, these funeral homes may also arrange for additional seating with closed-circuit television coverage. Likewise, many in the Indian community have incorporated practices such as visitations, eulogies, and displays of photos or videos of the deceased's life, which are not followed in India.

Losses and Tragedies in the Indian Community

The earliest record of a death in Minnesota's Indian community was in 1965, when *Sam Hooroo*, a graduate student at the University of Minnesota, died after a surgery. He was a Christian, so he was buried here, and the Indian community, with help from the International Students Office, sent his belongings and an album of photographs to his family in India.

In 1972, a sailor on an Indian freighter became ill and was admitted to St. Mary's Hospital in Duluth, where he died. When notified by a pastor at the hospital, members of the Indian community brought his body to the Twin Cities, helped with the cremation, and sent the ashes back to India.

In 1995, a young professional, *Vaidyanathan Krishnan*, drowned in the Mississippi as he was exploring the river, unaware that ice sheets formed over running water are not safe. His friends from the Indian community came together and, along with his employer, helped raise funds to ship his remains to India and to close and settle his bank accounts and property.

In 2007 and 2017, two young women, nineteen and twenty years old, died in car accidents that could have been prevented, devastating their families and throwing those who knew them into shock and grief. Both families have channeled their pain in positive directions by creating

In May 1973, graduate student Ram Nigam was killed by a stray bullet in a freak accident on a Minnesota freeway. His death traumatized the Indian community. Coordinating with the International Students Office, which helped with expenses, his friends sent his body back to his parents in Kanpur, India. *Courtesy Raj Saraf*

LEFT Shreya Dixit. *Photo by Michael's Studio*

RIGHT Ria Patel. *Courtesy the Ria Patel Foundation*

foundations in the women's memories and continue to heal by organizing awareness and educational programs to prevent future tragedies.

Shreya Dixit was coming home from college for the weekend in 2011 when the driver of the car in which she was the passenger got distracted and crashed into a concrete pillar, killing Shreya. The family poured their grief into establishing the Shreya R. Dixit Memorial Foundation, working tirelessly since her death to raise awareness of the hazards of distracted driving. They engage with legislators, driving schools, and students and use film, social media, and events such as the annual Raksha Walk to promote distraction-free driving. Shreya's father, Vijay, also published a highly researched solution-based book: *One Split Second: The Distracted Driving Epidemic, How It Kills and How We Can Fix It.*

Ria Patel was a passenger in a car whose driver was under the influence of alcohol and crashed the car, killing her. Family and friends launched the Ria Patel Foundation in May 2018 to bring attention to the hazards of distracted and drunk driving. The foundation has held events with others such as Toward Zero Deaths. Ria was a talented dancer, and in September 2018, a local Indian dance company, R. G. K. Dance, donated the entire proceeds of its show to the foundation.

6 Spotlighting Segments of the Indian Populations

As part of the fuller story of Indian American immigrants in Minnesota, it is helpful to consider the unique experiences and characteristics of specific segments of the population. This section highlights women, children (the second generation), seniors, and those who identify as part of the LGBTQ+ community.

WOMEN: PRESERVING TRADITION AND MAKING STRIDES IN THE MODERN WORLD

As mentioned in the story of the first wave of immigrants (see page 11), most Indians in Minnesota in the early years were students and men. While a few women may have been part of this group, it was only in the 1960s and early '70s, as these men began to marry and settle down in Minnesota, that many women began to arrive. The experiences of these early women differ from that of those who came later, and there has also been a noticeable shift in roles from traditional to modern.

Many, if not all, who arrived in the early years were educated and could, with varying abilities, speak English. Landing in Minnesota as young brides after a quickly arranged marriage, they had to get acquainted not only with a new culture but also with their husbands.

"It was December 25 at 12, midnight, 1970, when I landed at the Minneapolis airport. The first thing was I didn't know my husband very well. All the while on the plane I was thinking about my family who I had left. It was really a strange feeling; Where am I coming? What is ahead of me? I wasn't sure."

Aparna Ganguli, Oral History Project 1, India Association of Minnesota

Pursuing the typical immigrant dreams of success, many chose to go back to college to further their education and a few started working right away. Several, especially those who grew up in more conservative families and with traditional Indian values about masculine roles, assumed all housework responsibilities. Since Indian

"I was very popular and got invited to a lot of parties," says Geeta Vora, who was single when she came to Minnesota in the early 1970s. In those years, a woman arriving alone was not common as parents were reluctant to send their unmarried daughters abroad. Now it is not unusual for single Indian women to come on their own. Many arrive here as students or are sent by their employers to work on projects for Minnesota companies.
Courtesy Raj Saraf

ingredients were hard to find, they devised methods and recipes to substitute with what was available from American grocery stores.

When children were born, some mothers chose to stay home to raise their kids, while others, especially those with professional degrees, navigated daycare and babysitting options. All parents of young children had to learn how to raise them without the support system of the extended family they had left behind in India. Later, these women took newcomers under their wings, especially those from their own language, religious, or social groups.

Regardless of when they came to Minnesota, Indian women are generally the family's primary caregivers and preservationists of Indian culture. Many feel strongly that their children should grow up with Indian values and traditions and make efforts to practice and enforce them at home. Through networks of friends and by sharing information, they involve their children in similar activities. In multigenerational homes, they care for elders. Also, like most other women in the broader community, Indian women tend to maintain their family's social calendars, extending the well-known Indian hospitality by hosting dinner parties and organizing social events (see page 39).

Most Indian women have also kept up the tradition of wearing Indian attire and take immense pride in dressing in Indian clothes, especially on special occasions and in Indian gatherings. Women who arrived in the early years were more comfortable in the traditional saree, which was not practical during Minnesota's winters. In later years, many, especially second-generation Indian women, switched to wearing mostly Western clothing and were often reluctant to wear Indian attire in public. In recent times, especially as Minnesota's population becomes more diverse, a resurgence of this pride and comfort in wearing Indian clothes is evident, even with the second generation.

Over the years, traditional Indian gender roles have also evolved, especially among educated and working women who have become equal partners with their husbands. With easy access to information, the ability to drive, and economic means, many Indian women have become more independent, facing fewer traditional boundaries and voicing their opinions confidently.

Indian woman in Minnesota, like the men, have made great strides with their careers and are making outstanding contributions in their fields (see pages 102–20). They are doctors, engineers, and scientists, as well as educators and leaders at universities and colleges and in the K-12 schools. Some have climbed corporate ladders and hold executive positions in large companies. Many are entrepreneurs and own large and small businesses. Others work in retail and run home-based businesses offering services such as tailoring, beauty regimens, catering, and traditional practices such as yoga, Ayurveda medicine, and alternative therapies. In fact, 40 percent of Indian women are self-employed, contributing to 20 percent of the revenue earned by self-employed Indians. Among the second generation especially, many hold important positions in various government offices.

Unfortunately, despite all these positive developments, there have been incidents of domestic abuse in the Indian community. In recent years, organizations such as

SEWA-AIFW and AshaUSA (see page 68) have been established to provide cultur-ally sensitive help. Divorces are not common among Indians in Minnesota (only 3.3 percent of marriages end in divorce), but they are occurring despite the stigma. Marriages are sacrosanct in India, and until recently Indian women have shied away from divorces because of the emotional aftermath of breaking with tradition.

SECOND GENERATION: BALANCING TWO CULTURES

Children of parents who immigrated from India to the United States are often referred to as second-generation Indians. This category includes not just the ones born here but also those who were born in India and came to Minnesota when they were young. Depending on when they were born or immigrated and how strongly Indian traditions and lifestyles were enforced at home, their experiences differ. How-ever, one thing they all share is evident from the narrators who were interviewed for the Oral History Phase 2 Program by the Minnesota Historical Society: they have had to straddle two cultures more intensely than their parents.

While experiencing the same growing pains as their peers in the broader com-munity, they have had the added burden of adjusting to being different. Many mentioned that their behavior in schools or workplaces was markedly distinct from the way they acted with family: being "all-American" in the outside world and then adjusting their behavior at home to varying degrees, depending on the norms set by their parents. These differences range from food choices, languages spoken, and clothing worn to values and traditions. Many indulge in some form of *code-switching*, a linguistic term that refers to how one talks and behaves depending on where one is and with whom one is interacting.

Those who grew up when there were few Indians in Minnesota had dissimilar experiences from those who came in the 1970s, '80s, and later. Their parents were pioneering new parenting styles without the benefit of any support groups. Likewise, the children had fewer religious or cultural organizations or Indian schools in which to hang out with others like themselves. They had to endure the pressure of being conspicuous because in those years Minnesota's population was not as diverse, and their peers did not see many different people. Some recall crying and wanting to change their Indian names. Many felt confused and not sure where they belonged.

Those with one non-Indian parent had other experiences, depending on

"When I was a teenager and young adult, one of the hardest things about being a second-generation Indian American was that I didn't have anyone to model myself after—I didn't see women older than me who already had successfully navigated the experience of falling between Indian and American cultures. Today, though, I also see that as a gift—it's pushed me to learn from and find connection with a broader and more varied spectrum of people. And it's helped me to resist defining myself by others' ideas of what it is to be Indian or to be American. Some-times, though, it still can be a little lonely to be part of this in-between generation."

Ramona Advani, who grew up in Minnesota in the 1970s and early '80s

how much they were exposed to Indian culture and if they were encouraged to socialize and participate in Indian activities. For those whose parents rejected American parenting styles, there were conflicts when it came to sleepovers, dating, or selecting careers that deviated from the ones seen as successful: engineering, medicine, or law.

Many second-generation Indians in Minnesota have followed their parents' footsteps into the medical, engineering, and science fields. Like Indian students in other states, second-generation Indians in Minnesota have excelled in academics, whether as merit scholars or Rhodes Scholars or by winning other prestigious scholarships. For example, Adhithya Anandaraj, an eighth grader at Roosevelt Middle School in Blaine, won the 2019 National Geographic GeoBee Minnesota State Competition. Some have been admitted into Ivy League colleges and made contributions to Minnesota (see pages 102–20). Others are finding success in fields like journalism, art, K-12 education, politics, business, music, dance, and the armed forces. Since Indian parents highly value learning and save for educational opportunities, most second-generation Indians have been able to attend college, at least for their undergraduate degrees, relatively debt-free.

As the community has grown in number, it has become easier for younger members to embrace their Indian identities. Since many families continue to visit India and are involved in various cultural activities, second-generation Indians feel that they have the best of both worlds.

Second-generation adults with families of their own increasingly expose their children to Indian culture but less frequently than their parents did; they are most likely to attend more pan-Indian events. While they may have lots of friends outside the Indian community, they keep in touch and socialize with their parents' Indian friends and their children, with whom they grew up. Some also have been involved with an organization called Network of Indian-American Professionals (NetIP).

Courtesy Shanti Sury

From Homecoming Royalty to Rhodes Scholars
Second-generation Indians in Minnesota have made significant strides in various areas.

Shruti Mathur (below) was crowned University of Minnesota's Homecoming Queen in 2001. Priya M. Sury (above), who graduated from Washington University in St. Louis summa cum laude in anthropology and Spanish, was named a Rhodes Scholar in 2011. She is currently studying for a medical degree at the University of Minnesota. Other Rhodes Scholars from Minnesota include Ishanaa Rambachan (1998) and Prerna Nadathur (2011).

Courtesy Ravi Desai

GROWING OLD IN MINNESOTA: SENIORS IN THE INDIAN COMMUNITY

Indian culture has a strong tradition of respecting elders. In India today, it is not uncommon to see households with multigenerational families living together. Many first-generation Indian Americans grew up with this tradition, and when they started

The 55+ group picnic.
Courtesy Sudhanshu Misra

settling in Minnesota, it was natural to sponsor their elderly parents to come and live with them.

The family reunification clause in the Immigration and Nationality Act of 1965 helped bring Indian parents to the United States. According to immigration statistics, immigrants admitted to the United States aged fifty years and older grew to 19.5 percent in 2008, compared to three percent between 1965 and 1977.

Most of these seniors came after retirement and after spending most of their lives in India. Just like their children, they have had to make huge adjustments and adapt to new lifestyles, but at an older age. While they may enjoy taking care of grandkids and cooking for the family, they have also dealt with isolation and loss of independence; a few have experienced abuse and neglect.

Those who came to the United States and to Minnesota in the 1960s and 1970s now make up another group of seniors in the Indian community. Members of this group have planned for their retirement. They travel, and many have sold their homes and moved into senior and assisted-living facilities.

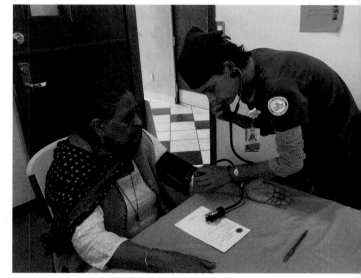

SEWA-AIFW (Asian Indian Family Wellness) organizes senior trips and runs a health clinic. *Courtesy SEWA-AIFW*

Some have decided to move out of Minnesota to be closer to their children. A few, like other seniors in Minnesota, have invested in second homes in warmer states such as Florida and Arizona. Others might spend the winter months in their hometowns in India.

As the need to help seniors has increased, particularly in cases of those who have come from India in their later years and those visiting children for the summer months, the community has come together to offer assistance. The India Association of Minnesota's 55+ group (now defunct) was one of the first formed to offer seniors organized activities such as lunches, picnics, and other outings.

SEWA–Asian Indian Family Wellness, AshaUSA, the Hindu Mandir, Geeta

Ashram, and other religious institutions organize monthly activities such as lunch gatherings and help with transportation. Organizations like SEWA-AIFW also conduct health camps and hold free health clinics at various community locations. These are staffed by culturally sensitive volunteer doctors who complete preliminary screenings and provide referrals and health resources to participants. Members of the community are discussing building assisted living and nursing homes that cater to the special needs of Indian seniors by providing services such as Indian food and aides who speak Indian languages.

INDIANS IN THE LGBTQ+ COMMUNITY: OVERCOMING THE STIGMA OF BEING DIFFERENT

In the early days, particularly in the 1970s and '80s, as in the larger society, there were no discussions on LGBTQ+ identities nor any known instances of anyone coming out in the Indian community. Later, even while their counterparts in India seemed to move on with the times, Indians in the United States tended to hold on to the more conservative view that was prevalent in India when they left. Fear of being rejected or bringing shame to their families prevented many from living their true identities. Years after LGBTQ+ identities became more acceptable in the broader society, some members of Minnesota's Indian community have started to come out and talk about their true selves.

One of the first to openly discuss his sexual orientation was *Raghavan Iyer*, a well-known author of several cookbooks, including *Betty Crocker's Indian Home Cooking*

Raghavan Iyer

Ameet. *Courtesy Dena Denny Photography*

(see page 120). While forging a career in the culinary field, he is open about being gay and living with his partner and their adopted son. While Raghavan grew up in a conservative South Indian family, they are accepting and supportive of him.

Ameet is an artist making a living as an independent consultant managing digital projects. He composes original material, has sung at various venues around the Twin Cities, has performed at Twin Cities Jazz Festival, and sings in the choir at Mount Olivet Church in Minneapolis.

Ameet came out in his twenties when the pressure of fielding marriage proposals sent by his parents from India became overwhelming. He says, "I did not want to live a lie; it got unbearable. Hinduism does not condemn homosexuality, and as a Hindu, I feel my sexual orientation is not just acceptable but celebrated." His parents, though accepting, still feel the societal pressure of "what people would say." Ameet grew up in Mumbai and came to the United States in 1995 to pursue a master's degree in computer science. He thinks that getting away from the Indian-male stereotype and coming to the United States helped him explore his orientation along with his art.

Milin Dutta always knew he was different. Born as a girl, he preferred dressing as a boy and doing things expected of a son. Growing up in India, he struggled with his feelings because of the way transgender people are treated and the lack of support. The process of becoming a trans man was slow and happened after he came to the United States as a software consultant in 1994 and got acquainted with the LGBTQ+ community. He first shared news about the change with his siblings and only in 2016 with his parents; all have been supportive.

Dutta is very active in the LGBTQ+ community in the Twin Cities, where he started a support group called Out in the Backyard, an LGBTQ cultural wellness center. He also organizes events to raise funds for youth activities in his hometown of Guwahati in Assam, India, and spends months at a time there organizing and supporting these efforts.

Milin Dutta. *Courtesy Geeti Das*

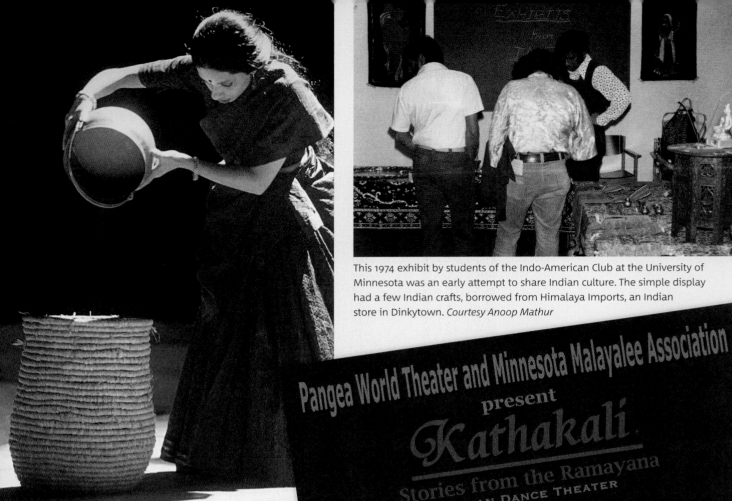

This 1974 exhibit by students of the Indo-American Club at the University of Minnesota was an early attempt to share Indian culture. The simple display had a few Indian crafts, borrowed from Himalaya Imports, an Indian store in Dinkytown. *Courtesy Anoop Mathur*

Nirupama Nityanadan (Rani) in the Guthrie Theater's 1993 production of *Naga Mandala* by Girish Karnad, directed by Garland Wright. *Photo by Michal Daniel*

In the 1980s, a group of dancers from diverse backgrounds performed the relatively unknown dances of the Munda tribe at various events in the Twin Cities. *Courtesy Gundu Rao*

Taking a cue from the opera, this classical dance drama presented by Pangea World Theater and the Minnesota Malayalee Association projected translated lyrics and close-ups of facial expressions to help the audience follow the plot of *Kathakali*. *Courtesy Godan Nambudiripad*

Pangea World Theater and Minnesota Malayalee Association
present
Kathakali
Stories from the Ramayana
INDIAN DANCE THEATER

MAY 7, 2005, 6:45 P.M.
AT PANTAGES THEATRE,
710 HENNEPIN AVENUE, MINNEAPOLIS, MN 554

7 Contributing to Minnesota

Indians in Minnesota, while preserving their roots and staying connected to their homeland, have also made and are continuing to make significant contributions to Minnesota's cultural, social, and political landscape as well as to its economy.

SHARING AND SHOWCASING INDIAN CULTURE

Indians are proud of their heritage, and many in the community enthusiastically share it individually as well as collectively through organized efforts. Performances by dance schools and other arts groups at events such as IndiaFest and the Festival of Nations have exposed other Minnesotans to India's diverse and rich culture.

Individuals from the community make presentations about India at schools, churches, libraries, and work sites. By explaining various aspects of their culture, they hope to educate members of the larger community and dispel stereotypes about India as well as instill in their children a sense of pride in their heritage.

Festival of Nations

Since 1979, Indians have participated in the annual Festival of Nations, a large event organized by the International Institute of Minnesota at the RiverCentre in St. Paul. India Association of Minnesota, the School of India for Languages and Culture, and other organizations and vendors represent Indian culture and food at the festival's cultural exhibits, international marketplace and bazaar, and children's and adult dance performances.

Newly married women dressed as brides took part in the 1972 Minnesota Aquatennial Festival. *Courtesy Sudha Arora*

Ayudha Puja or "worship of instruments of work" is a part of the Dussehra / Navratri festival. It is also called "Astra Puja". The puja focuses specific attention to one's profession and its related tools and connotes that a divine force is working with us helping to perform well and for obtaining the proper reward.

The Festival of Nations

India has been well represented at the Festival of Nations since 1979. India Association of Minnesota with the help of the School of India for Languages and Culture and other Indian organizations participate in many activities at this large international gathering. *Courtesy Gundu Rao, IAM, SILC, author*

IndiaFest

Since 1983, India Association of Minnesota (IAM) has been organizing an event that showcases the food, culture, and diversity of India. Its name has evolved from India Day to Festival of India to today's IndiaFest; it was first held in a high school in 1984, then moved to the Landmark Center in St. Paul in 1985, and since 2009 takes place on the Minnesota capitol grounds in St. Paul. The free festival draws thousands of people to view musical and dance performances, enjoy Indian food from local restaurants, shop, and learn about Indian organizations in Minnesota. The celebration kicks off with a parade, and a ceremony involves raising the flags of both India and the United States and speeches from elected officials and visiting dignitaries.

IndiaFest (India Day) through the years. *Courtesy IAM*

Nirmala Rajasekar and other musicians performing Carnatic music. Each year, the India Association of Minnesota and the School of India for Languages and Culture represent India at the Flint Hills International Children's Festival and other community gatherings. *Courtesy SILC*

Oral History Projects

In the 1990s, after Indian Americans had been settling in Minnesota for a few decades, Ram Gada and Godan Nambudiripad approached the Minnesota Historical Society to interview and record for posterity, as well as for research, a series of oral histories of individuals and organizations in the Indian community.

From 1993 to 2014, nine projects were completed. Many include not only interviews but also archived newsletters, meeting minutes, photographs, and recorded performances, all of great benefit to researchers. Many of these projects can be accessed online through the Minnesota Historical Society's website and through the library. Polly Sonnifer and Dan Rein conducted most of the interviews. The project is currently being managed by Raj Menon.

ORAL HISTORY PROJECT 1 (COMPILED 1993–95): Experiences of the earliest Asian Indian immigrants to Minnesota (1950s–60s), including sixteen people with diverse backgrounds of geographical regions, languages, religions, and customs.

> **Interviewees for Oral History Project 1** were M. J. Abhisekhar, Indru Advani, Pennamma Cherucheril, Ram Gada, Aparna Ganguli, Mansur Kassim-Lakha, P. C. Mangalick, Sudhansu Misra, Mahendra Nath, Vilma K. Patel, Ranee Ramaswamy, Kusum Saxena, Dr. Abul Hassan Siddiqui, Bash Singh, Sister Jancy, and Sister Tresa Jose.

ORAL HISTORY PROJECT 2 (1997–98): Experiences of fifteen children of early Asian Indian immigrants who were living in two cultures, Indian at home and American at school and work.

Interviewees of the first India Association of Minnesota oral history project (1993–95) with the Minnesota Historical Society. *MNHS*

Interviewees of the fourth India Association of Minnesota oral history project (2000–2001) with the Minnesota Historical Society. *MNHS*

Interviewees for Oral History Project 2 were Ramona Advani, Simi Ahuja, Satveer Chaudhary, Ina Ganguli, Alim Kassim, Suruchi Patankar Kelly, Geeta Saxena McGibbon, Nirupama Misra, Alli Naithani, Guptan Nambudiripad, Deepak Nath, Lisa Gada Norton, Aparna Ramaswamy, Rajiv Shah, and Vishant Shah.

ORAL HISTORY PROJECT 3 (1999–2000): Experiences of eight Indian Americans living outside the metro area, newly arrived technology experts helping companies prepare for Y2K, and immigrants who were adopted or moved to other parts of the world.

Interviewees for Oral History Project 3 were Lincoln Gada, Sunanda Iyengar, Ravinder Manku, Prasanna Mishra, Neelam Naik, Krishnan Nambudiripad, Nayana Ramakrishnan, Jonathan Remund, and Dr. Ved Sharma.

SCHOOL OF INDIA FOR LANGUAGES AND CULTURE ORAL HISTORY PROJECT (2000–2001): Included the founders, teachers, students, and officers of the School of India for Languages and Culture (SILC).

Interviewees for SILC Oral History Project were Ketan Gada, Neena Gada, Anoop Mathur, Preeti Mathur, Shruti Mathur, Manas Menon, Rajan Menon, Rita Mustaphi, Godan Nambudiripad, Rama Padmanabhan, Punjabhai Patel, Shanti Shah, and Chitra Subrahmanian.

ORAL HISTORY PROJECT 4 (2003–05): Included twelve people who narrated the growth of the India Association of Minnesota (IAM).

Interviewees for Oral History Project 4 were Jagdish Desai, Gummadi J. Franklin, Neena Gada, Dilip Mallick, Ashoke Mandal, Niru Misra, Sarat Mohapatra, Godan Nambudiripad, Stefan Peterson, Shanti Shah, Deep Shikha, and Vasant Sukhatme.

ORAL HISTORY PROJECT (2010–11): Included narrators from the Indian Music Society of Minnesota. IMSOM and the Minnesota Historical Society archived 160 digitized musical concerts of visiting musicians to Minnesota going back more than thirty years.

Interviewees for this Oral History Project were Dr. Jay Jayraman, Dr. Amita Kelekar, Dr. A. Pavan, Krishna Prasad, Dr. V. Premanand, Nayana Ramakrishnan, S. Ramakrishnan, and Cliff Sloane.

ORAL HISTORY PROJECT (2012–13): Included narrators from the Ragamala Dance Company. Ragamala and the Minnesota Historical Society archived more than twenty years of digitized dance performances.

Interviewees for this Oral History Project were Jeff Bartlett, Tamara Nadel, Godan Nambudiripad, Aparna Ramaswamy, Ashwini Ramaswamy, Ranee Ramaswamy, Louise Robinson, and Cliff Sloane.

ORAL HISTORY PROJECT (2012-13): Included narrators from the Katha Dance Theatre.

Interviewees for this Oral History Project were Vicki Benson, Frances Boehnlein, Marcia Boehnlein, Bob Burns, Daniel Gabriel, Sangeeta Jain, Myron Johnson, Pandit Birju Maharaj, Dayna Martinez, Patricia A. Mitchel, Kalyan Mustaphi, Rita Mustaphi, Pooja Newcom, Derek Phillips, Shelley Quiala, Robert Robinson, Guru Saswati Sen, Asha Sharma, Cliff Sloane, and Sharon Varosh.

ORAL HISTORY PROJECT (2013-14): Included narrators from the Hindu Society of Minnesota.

Interviewees for this Oral History Project were Vishal Agarwal, Sushumna Tandon Aggarwal, Anandi Balasubramanian, Raj Balasubramanian, Murali Bhattar, Annika Borgaonkar, Byron Byraiah, Mythili Chari, Dr. Vaddu Chari, Dr. S. K. Dash, Kanak Dutt, Ram Gada, Punjabhai Patel, Nayana Ramakrishnan, Dr. Kumud Sane, Dr. Shashikant Sane, Dr. Krishna Mohan Saxena, Dr. Kusum Saxena, and Narender Venkata.

OPPOSITE A special program to inaugurate the *Beyond Bollywood* exhibition featured cultural performances including a veena performance by Nirmala Rajasekar, a local artist of international repute. *MNHS*

Beyond Bollywood Exhibit

Beyond Bollywood: Indian Americans Shape the Nation, created by the Smithsonian's Asian Pacific American Center and the Smithsonian Institution Traveling Exhibition Service, was on view April 30 through July 10, 2016, at the Minnesota History Center.

It was the first time an exhibit of this scale was held to document and showcase the history and culture of Indians in the United States. The Minnesota Historical Society enhanced and localized the exhibit with several panels documenting the sixty years of experiences and contributions of the Indian community in Minnesota. Several cultural and family events hosted at the History Center during the exhibition period brought many Minnesotans to view the exhibit and learn about the community. An advisory committee of Indian Americans in Minnesota, along with significant financial contributions from several individuals, made it possible to shape this exhibit and bring it to Minnesota.

GIVING BACK THROUGH PHILANTHROPY AND VOLUNTEERING

Individual efforts include:
Donating and cooking in soup kitchens
Visiting and helping in nursing homes
Teaching and coaching underprivileged students in science and math
Helping sew and make quilts
Working in food shelves
Volunteering in children's schools and with various sports teams and other extracurricular activities
Volunteering and serving in various professional societies
Volunteering through organizations such as Rotary and Lion's Club

Indians have a strong sense of responsibility and believe in giving back to the community where they are living, raising their families, and enjoying opportunities. Indians Americans—whether firmly established or recently arrived—have looked for many ways to give back, both as individual volunteers and through collective efforts arranged by various Indian and non-Indian organizations.

beyond BOLLYWOOD

INDIAN AMERICANS SHAPE THE NATION

In the western imagination, India conjures up many things: elephants, saris, and spices; gurus, gods, and goddesses; turbans, temples, and a billion faces drawn from ancient and modern history; and the pulsating energy of Bollywood movies.

But in America, India's contributions stretch far beyond these stereotypes.

The story begins with Indian sailors employed on British ships who traveled to the United States as early as the 1790s. Indian traders of silk, spices, and other fine items soon followed. This story includes workers who built railroads and families who formed the backbone of California's farms. The first Asian in Congress. The creator of Hotmail. Athletes. Doctors. Cab drivers. Musicians. Activists.

Today, one out of every 100 Americ... her roots to India. From Silicon Valle... U.S.A., the lives and stories of Ameri... Indian Americans are woven into the... this nation—and have shaped what i...

Created by the Smithsonian Asian Pacific Ameri... Smithsonian Institution Traveling Exhibition Serv...

Designed, edited, and produced by the Smithson...

This small community provides us a constant reminder that immigrants continue to propel Minnesota to newer frontiers and unimaginable possibilities.
—Bruce Corrie, 2015

A few group volunteer efforts:

The nonprofit *Are You Hungry* was started in January 2016 by Senthilkumar Ramamoorthy when he saw a veteran standing on Highway 55 in cold weather asking for food. Since then, Ramamoorthy has mobilized a large group of people to help the hungry. They donate food and clothing to the homeless through various agencies as well as on the streets. The team also cooks and serves in soup kitchens. *Courtesy Are You Hungry*

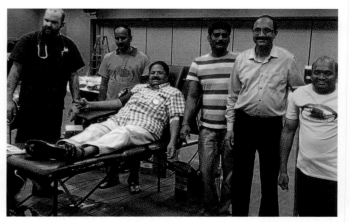

Blood drive at the Hindu Mandir, part of the outreach program Hindu Sewa Diwas, or Hindu Service Day. *Courtesy Hindu Mandir*

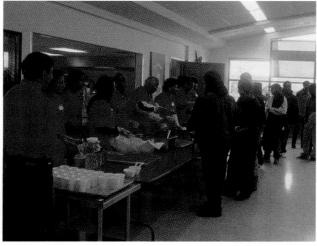

Members of the Hindu Mandir regularly cook and serve vegetarian meals at the Dorothy Day Center in St. Paul and House of Charity in Minneapolis. They often use offerings of rice and lentils made at the temple to prepare the soup for the hungry. *Courtesy Hindu Mandir*

Foundations and other programs established by Indian Americans in Minnesota include:

Adopt a Senior. A program through the India Association of Minnesota that involves visiting nursing homes and befriending seniors.

Athletes Committed to Educating Students (ACES). A Twin Cities organization that helps reduce the academic gap among underserved students, founded in 1994 by Dr. Rajiv Shah.

CAPI USA. Formerly known as the Centre for Asian and Pacific Islanders, this organization helps refugees and immigrants gain access to jobs, housing, food, health education, and social services to promote economic independence, self-determination, and social equality. CAPI USA's executive director is Ekta Prakash.

Compassionate Action for Animals. This animal advocacy organization was cofounded in 1998 by Unny Nambudiripad and organizes the annual Veg Fest to encourage adoption of a plant-based diet.

Dr. Dash Foundation. Helping to preserve and promote Indian heritage, education, research, innovation, and health care through efforts in Minnesota as well as with Indian organizations throughout the world.

Education Foundation. Established by Dr. Krishna M. Saxena and Dr. Kusum Saxena at Children's Hospital.

Nath Foundation. Established by Mahendra Nath to fund Normandale Community College in Bloomington, the Hindu Mandir, and other organizations.

Out In the Backyard—Cultural Wellness Center. Established by Milin Dutta in 2012 and focusing on LGBTQ+ issues to build a healthy community.

Dr. S. K. and Kalpana Dash, of the Dr. Dash Foundation, which has supported organizations focused on health, education, and culture, including AshaUSA, SEWA, Vidya Gyan, the Hindu Society of Minnesota, the India Association of Minnesota, the Odisha Society of Minnesota, the Minnesota Historical Society, and numerous dance and theater groups.

Dr. V. Premanand Theatre and Concert Hall and scholarships at Normandale Community College, Bloomington. Dr. Jayaseetha Premanand and the late Dr. Visvanatha Premanand have made extensive contributions in support of education.

Reddy Foundation. Established by Madhu Reddy to enhance the dignity and well-being of socially and economically vulnerable people.

Ria Patel Foundation. Helping to eradicate distracted driving (see page 82).

Shreya R. Dixit Memorial Foundation. Building distraction-free driver communities (see page 82).

Vora S.E.R.V.I.C.E. Established in 2014 by Dr. Geeta Vora to increase the graduation rate for youth coming from low-income families by providing real-time mentoring designed to keep children in school.

Madhu and Dr. Jyothsna Reddy, Reddy Foundation

Members of the Indian American community in Minnesota, like their counterparts in other regions of the United States, are high achievers who have been extremely successful in their chosen fields and businesses. To illustrate how this immigrant group has been contributing to Minnesota, this section profiles a few community members to represent the various fields.

Political Action and Government and Public Service

Nearly a quarter (23.4 percent) of Indians in Minnesota are naturalized citizens. Many are increasingly getting involved in politics—locally and nationally. The Asian Indian American Republicans of Minnesota and Minnesota Asian Indian Democratic Association (MAIDA) were established in 1992 and 1994, respectively, to encourage Indian Americans to participate in the US political process.

Asian Indian American Republicans of Minnesota founders include Gopal Khanna, Vijay Bala Krishnan, Lata Setty, and Dr. Vijay Sood.

Minnesota Asian Indian Democratic Association founders include Satveer Chaudhary, Neena Gada, Prema Nadig, and Seshaaiyar Ramakrishnan.

During elections, citizens campaign for their chosen candidates, attend caucuses, and even represent Minnesota at national conventions. Many Indians volunteer as election judges and attend election night get-togethers to watch returns at local party headquarters.

Additionally, Indian Americans, particularly of the second generation, are involved in government roles and in public service fields, contributing at national, state, and city levels.

Senator Amy Klobuchar with members of the Indian community at the Minnesota Asian Indian Democratic Association (MAIDA) booth at IndiaFest, 2017. *Courtesy IAM*

Dr. Ravi Chaudhary is the Director of Advanced Programs and Innovation for the Office of Commercial Space at the Federal Aviation Administration. He is a member of the federal government's

Ananth Shankar at the Democratic National Convention in 2016. *Courtesy Ananth Shankar*

Members of the India Association of Minnesota at the Coalition of Asian American Leaders (CAAL) at the Minnesota State Capitol, April 1, 2019. *Courtesy Anoop Mathur*

Paul Wellstone met with Indians at India Day at the Landmark Center, October 6, 2002. *Courtesy Raj Menon*

On November 17, 2001, the Indian community in Minnesota held an interfaith prayer service at the state capitol rotunda and presented funds for victims of the 9/11 attacks. Members of the community stand with secretary of state Mary Kiffmeyer, state senator Satveer Chaudhary, and St. Paul mayor Randy Kelly. *Courtesy Indian Reporter*

Senior Executive Service, making him the highest-ranking Indian American federal employee from Minnesota. In 2014, Dr. Chaudhary was appointed by President Barack Obama as a member of the President's Advisory Commission on Asian Americans and Pacific Islanders. Focusing on service and care for veterans, his tenure was continued under the Trump administration. A former air force officer, Chaudhary completed twenty-one years of military service. He has logged more than three thousand hours as a pilot and flight test engineer, including 760 combat hours. His honors include the NASA Stellar Award, Meritorious Service Medal, Air Medal, and Iraq and Afghanistan Campaign Medals.

Dr. Ravi Chaudhary

Satveer Chaudhary was the first Indian American senator in US history. He was also the first Asian American in the Minnesota legislature, and only the fourth Indian American elected to any office in the United States. First elected at age twenty-seven,

Satveer Chaudhary

Ramona Advani (second generation) is general counsel and deputy state auditor for Minnesota's Office of the State.

Chaudhary served in the Minnesota House from 1997 to 2001 and Senate from 2001 to 2011. Representing northern suburbs of Minneapolis and St. Paul, Senator Chaudhary helped pass laws improving public safety, the environment, education, employment rights, and health care. A graduate of St. Olaf College and the University of Minnesota Law School, Chaudhary continues to fight for the community as an immigration attorney.

Sangeeta Jain is a Fourth Judicial District court referee in Hennepin County, a child support magistrate, a law professor with Hamline University School of Law in St. Paul, and a mediator and facilitator with the Minnesota Department of Education. Jain served as a staff attorney with the Minnesota Justice Foundation from 2002 to 2003, as an assistant Ramsey County attorney from 1994 to 1999, and as a staff attorney with Legal Aid Society in Minneapolis in 1994. She earned a master of laws degree from the University of San Diego Law School in 1989, a juris doctorate degree from Hamline University in 1988, and a bachelor of arts degree from the University of Minnesota in 1985.

Gopal Khanna served as the director of the Agency for Healthcare Research and Quality in President Donald Trump's administration. Under Governor Tim Pawlenty, he served as Minnesota's first chief information officer (CIO) and was also the lead cochair of the nineteen-member Minnesota Commission on Service Innovation (CSI). Under President George W. Bush, he held several senior policy positions, including CIO and chief financial officer (CFO) of the Peace Corps and CFO of the president's office of administration.

In 2006, following President George W. Bush's nomination, *Rachel Paulose* became the first Indian American US attorney to be unanimously confirmed by the US Senate. She served in this role until November 2007 and later worked as senior counsel at the Securities and Exchange Commission.

Gopal Khanna

Rachel Paulose

Neel Kashkari

Bruce Corrie

Two second-generation Indian Americans, *Neel Kashkari* and *Narayana Rao Kocherlakota*, became president of the Federal Reserve Bank of Minneapolis. In 2018, *Bruce Corrie* was appointed director of planning and economic development by St. Paul mayor Melvin Carter. *P. G. Narayanan* served the Eden Prairie City Council as chair of the Human Rights and Diversity Commission.

P. G. Narayanan

Ram Gada served on the Minnesota Historical Society's executive council as board member and vice president (2003–12) and was elected honorary council member in 2016—the first Asian and Indian American to be celebrated in this way for public service. He also received a lifetime service award from the Council on Asian Pacific Minnesotans in 2014.

Military Service

Indian Americans from Minnesota have served the nation with valor and distinction in conflicts dating back to World War II, when *Mohan Singh Sekhon* served as an army doctor stationed in France. Since the 1970s, Indian Americans from Minnesota have contributed in greater numbers, with service representation in nearly every conflict the nation has been involved in.

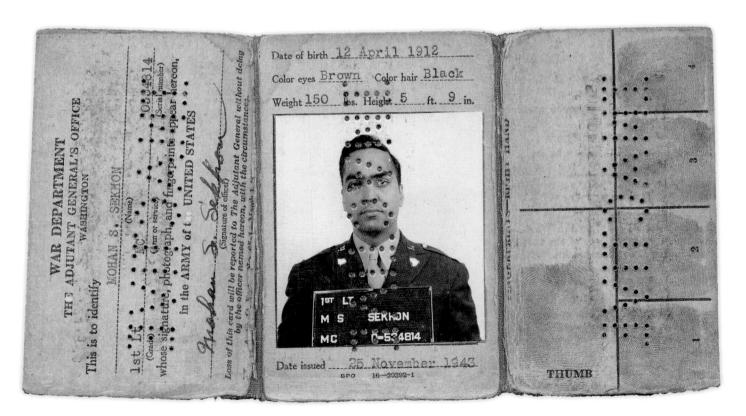

Dr. Mohan Sekhon, the earliest known Indian American in Minnesota, served as an army doctor in World War II. *Courtesy Sylvia Sekhon*

Sanjai Kumar graduated from West Point in the 1970s, the first Indian American from Minnesota to graduate from a military service academy. He served as a helicopter pilot in the army and later in the US Department of State. *Colonel Varun Puri* graduated from the Air Force Academy in 1995 and attained the highest military rank by an Indian American from Minnesota. He served as a fighter pilot, flew combat missions over Kosovo, and was selected for duty at the elite Air Force Test Pilot School. He later served in key roles at the Pentagon, leading the development of all new fighter programs for the air force. *Lieutenant Colonel Aarti Puri* graduated from the Air Force Academy in 2001 and completed combat deployments in support of Operation Enduring Freedom. Deployed almost immediately after September 11, 2001, *Lieutenant Colonel Ravi Chaudhary* flew more than 150 combat missions over Iraq and Afghanistan as a transport pilot, delivering critical troops and cargo into combat zones, as well as key classified missions.

Parag Desai was a C-12 instructor pilot for the US Army and is now a first officer for United Airlines. In twenty-five years with the army, Desai served two tours in Iraq.

J. Ashwin Madia joined the US Marine Corps and served as judge advocate. In 2005, he was deployed to Iraq and worked with the State Department, the Justice Department, the United Nations, the European Union, and Iraqi judges and attorneys to help establish the rule of law in Iraq.

Parag Desai

J. Ashwin Madia

Several second-generation Indian Boy Scouts have attained the Eagle Scout rank, including Sujan Kamran and Ashwin Kamath. Troop 609 in Shoreview had five Indian American Eagle Scouts, including Mohan Pai, Naveen Pai, Vinay Pai, and Sujan Mathur. *Courtesy author*

Minal Sahu Parikh is a civilian trooper with the Bloomington Police, where she is training with the bomb squad and other units. *Courtesy Minal Sahu Parikh*

Yoga, Meditation, and Alternative Medicine and Healing

Yoga and meditation are India's gifts to the Western world, where these practices have been embraced and popularized since the 1960s. In Minnesota, there are many centers run by non-Indians, but the following were originally started by or are currently run by Indians.

Meditation Center. At one of the oldest meditation centers in Minnesota, located in Northeast Minneapolis, teachers focus on the Himalayan meditation practice. Started in 1968, it was led for many years by Dr. Usharbudh Arya (Swami Veda Bharati), who came to teach Sanskrit at the University of Minnesota.

Minneapolis Meditation Group of Self-Realization Fellowship. Part of a religious society that was founded by Paramahansa Yogananda, this center in south Minneapolis offers meditation and energizing classes.

Science of Spirituality Meditation Center. This center, founded by Arvind Naik and located in Northeast Minneapolis, is part of a spiritual organization started by Sant Rajinder Singh and dedicated to using meditation for personal transformation.

Alternative medicine and healing teachers and practitioners
Asavari Manvikar, yoga teacher and Ayurvedic doctor
Mukta Mudgal, Ayurvedic practitioner and meditation teacher
Prema Mysore, energy healing, yogic and Ayurvedic lifestyle practitioner and teacher
Leela Ugargol, energy healer, Reiki master, and past life analyzer

Punjabhai Patel has taught yoga for more than forty years in the Twin Cities—at the School of India for Languages and Culture, at community centers, and at the Hindu temple. *Courtesy SILC*

Yoga teachers. Many practitioners from the Indian community teach yoga at a place of worship such as the Hindu temple or offer private classes (see page 52).

Alternative medicine and healing teachers and practitioners. In recent years, as interest in alternative health care benefits grows, a few Indian Americans have started to explore and offer help with ancient practices such as Ayurveda and energy healing.

Yoga teachers
Mythili Chari, yoga instructor
Alpa Goswami, yoga instructor
Gita Kar, yoga and meditation instructor
Vinita Khatavkar, registered yoga instructor
Abhay Ladhe, Art of Living teacher
Punjabhai Patel, yoga instructor

Technology, Scientists, and Inventors

As scientists and engineers, many Indian Americans have contributed to Minnesota companies such as 3M, Medtronic, and Honeywell. Indian American scientists and engineers hold patents and have conducted groundbreaking research, and several have won the highest technical awards offered by their companies.

Babu N. Gaddam is a corporate scientist at the Corporate Research Materials Laboratory for 3M, where he has worked since 1985. Specializing in organic polymer synthesis and structure-property of polymers, he has earned numerous awards and has been issued 154 patents. He has taught at the University of St. Thomas, at the University of Minnesota, and at 3M.

Babu N. Gaddam

Indian Americans have been awarded patents for their inventions and are top performers for their respective companies, winning their highest awards. *Courtesy author*

Sumitra Mitra

Dr. Raj V. Rajan

Shantanu Sarkar

Jayshree Seth

A polymer scientist by training, *Sumita Mitra* worked at 3M Company for thirty-two years and was the industrial director of Minnesota Dental Research Center for Biomaterials and Biomechanics at the University of Minnesota for ten years. Her inventions in nanocomposites, adhesives, and resin-modified glass ionomers have been translated into innovative products that have transformed the practice of dentistry. She has one hundred US patents and, in 2018, was inducted into the National Inventors Hall of Fame.

An environmental engineer, *Dr. Raj V. Rajan* is active in global industry groups focused on climate change and water pollution; has served as an advisor in public-sector international and national guidance, research, and teaching institutions; serves on the boards of nonprofits shaping the region's clean energy and environmental policies; and was appointed by Governor Mark Dayton to the Minnesota Clean Water Council.

Several Indians received Honeywell's highest technical achievement, the Harold W. Sweatt Award. Here are the ones from Minnesota who were recognized for their outstanding contributions:
C. S. Reddy (1974)
Pat M. Narendra (1978)
Anil Jain; Durga P. Panda (1981)
Akbar Saffari (1986)
Mahesh Jeerage (1989)
Bharat Pant (1992)
Anoop Mathur (1997)
Dinkar Mylaraswamy (1998)

Shantanu Sarkar is a senior principal scientist at Medtronic, where he has helped develop algorithms for atrial fibrillation detection and for heart failure risk identification and disease management in pacemaker, defibrillator, and cardiac resynchronization therapy devices. He was named a Medtronic technical fellow and a Bakken fellow, has thirty issued patents, and earned the Medtronic Patent of Distinction award. He holds a PhD in biomedical engineering from the University of Minnesota.

Jayshree Seth is a corporate scientist at 3M and leads applied technology development projects for the Industrial Adhesives and Tapes Division, the company's largest industrial business. She holds sixty-five US patents for a variety of innovations, including adhesives, tapes, nonwovens, and fasteners. She is also a certified Design for Six Sigma Black Belt. As 3M's first-ever Chief Science Advocate, Seth seeks to make science more accessible and to foster a new generation of scientists and science advocates.

Management/Executives

Many Indian Americans have climbed corporate ladders and are in management and executive positions. The number of Indian Americans in management positions rose from 7.2 percent in 1990 to 17.8 percent in 2017. Several are featured elsewhere in this chapter. Here is a success story of a second-generation Indian.

Paurvi Bhatt is the vice president of Medtronic Philanthropy and president of the Medtronic Foundation. A seasoned global health and development leader, she has worked with companies, in government positions, and in the nonprofit sector to deliver innovative solutions in strategic philanthropy and investment; corporate social responsibility; health benefit reimbursement; and partnership design, particularly in emerging markets and resource-poor settings. She serves on advisory groups and boards focusing on women's leadership and global health.

Medicine and Health Care

About 11.3 percent of Indians work in medical fields, serving as doctors, surgeons, specialists, and educators at the Mayo Clinic, the University of Minnesota, and other hospitals and clinics. Many are well known nationally and internationally for contributions in their fields.

Paurvi Bhatt

Dr. Kumar G. Belani is the distinguished International Professor of Health at the University of Minnesota. He received the UMN President's Award for Outstanding Service and was inducted into the Academy for Excellence in Health Care Practice. He is the president of the Society for Ambulatory Anesthesia and is the pediatric anesthesiologist-in-chief. Dr. Belani is responsible for establishing medical and other academic relationships between the University of Minnesota and several institutions in India.

Dr. Badrinath Konety serves as chief executive officer of University of Minnesota Physicians as well as vice dean for Clinical Affairs at the University of Minnesota Medical School. He is a professor in the department of urology and director of the Institute for Prostate and Urologic Cancers. Dr. Konety has published more than 120 peer-reviewed articles, as well as a number of book chapters and review articles. Recognized as an expert on prostate and bladder cancer, he has been awarded multiple grants and has given presentations on a wide range of urologic oncology topics nationally and internationally.

Dr. Kumar G. Belani

Dr. Vibhu Kshettry is a researcher at the Minneapolis Heart Institute Foundation and a cardiovascular, thoracic, and cardiac transplant surgeon at Abbott Northwestern Hospital's Minneapolis Heart Institute. He has also served as director of the institute and as director of its Mechanical Cardiac Assist Program and its Cardiovascular Integrated Health Services.

Dr. Vibhu Kshettry

Dr. Ramaiah Muthyala is a research associate professor and director of the Department of Experimental and Clinical Pharmacology at the University of Minnesota. He

Minnesota ranks number two in percentage of doctors born in India (six percent). Although many Indian doctors serve in urban areas, they also help ease the region's shortage of rural family physicians. Since the mid-1970s, small towns like Crookston and Thief River Falls have relied on Indian doctors.

received the Lifetime Achievement Award from the India Association of Minnesota in recognition of his outstanding work on awareness and policy advocacy for rare diseases for the Asian Indian community. "This award is a testament that the Asian Indian community in Minnesota recognizes that rare diseases issues are social issues and affect all nationalities," said Dr. Muthyala, who is also president and CEO of the Indian Organization for Rare Diseases.

Dr. Kumud Sane and Dr. Shashikant Sane

Dr. Kusum Saxena and Dr. Krishna Saxena

Dr. Shashikant Sane (diagnostic radiology) and *Dr. Kumud Sane* (pediatric endocrinology) and *Dr. Kusum Saxena* (toxicology and emergency medicine) and *Dr. Krishna Saxena* (pediatric endocrinology) have lived in Minnesota for more than fifty years and have contributed many years of service in their respective areas of expertise. They have been involved community leaders as well, largely with establishing the Hindu Society of Minnesota and its temple.

Dr. Rajiv Shah

Dr. Rajiv Shah (second generation) is a nephrologist with Fairview Health Services. He earned his medical degree from the University of Minnesota and also completed his fellowship there. Dr. Shah is the founder of ACES (see page 100).

Dr. Amit Sood, formerly director of research in the Complementary and Integrative Medicine Program and chair of the Mind-Body Medicine Initiative at Mayo Clinic in Rochester, is a world-leading expert in resilience and stress management. He is also the researcher and creator behind the Mayo Clinic Resilient Mind program and has authored multiple books, including *The Mayo Clinic Guide to Stress-Free Living* and *The Mayo Clinic Handbook for Happiness*. Dr. Sood's innovative approach toward resilience incorporates concepts from neuroscience, evolutionary biology, psychology, philosophy, and biomedical research.

Dr. Amit Sood

Dr. Krishnan Subrahmanian (second generation) is a pediatrician with Hennepin Healthcare, also specializing in tropical medicine, HIV/AIDS, and global child health.

He is actively involved in establishing a health delivery system at the Pine Ridge Reservation in South Dakota. In 2008, Dr. Subrahmanian managed President Barack Obama's primaries in five states.

Dr. Krishnan Subrahmanian

The Arts

Minnesota is home to many award-winning Indian American artists whose prolific performances and unique multicultural collaborations have shone in the state's art and theater scenes, exposing Minnesotans to Indian dance, theater, and music (see pages 60–65).

Other artists and professionals:
Pujan Gandhi, Jane Emison Assistant Curator of South and Southeast Asian Art, Minneapolis Institute of Art
Pratibha Gupta, painting
Shakun Maheshwari, painting: henna and rangoli (floor painting)
Thanuja Namboodiripad, painting
Dr. Bharat Pant, painting
Kesavan Potti, painting

Education

Since Indians came to Minnesota primarily for education, it is not surprisingly that a large number of them are employed in a variety of academic fields as professors, researchers, and administrators at various institutions of higher learning. This impressive number also includes several Indian women, like *Ameeta Jaiswal-Dale* (associate professor, finance, University of St. Thomas), *Indira Junghare* (professor, Asian and Middle Eastern studies, University of Minnesota), *Anupama Pasricha* (department chair/associate professor, apparel design, fashion, merchandising, St. Catherine University), and *Deep Shikha* (chair/professor, economics and political science, St. Catherine University). Here are profiles of a few Indian Americans in academia.

V. V. Chari is the Paul Frenzel Land Grant Professor of Liberal Arts in the University of Minnesota's department of economics, the founding director of the university's Heller-Hurwicz Economics Institute, and an adviser at the Federal Reserve Bank of Minneapolis. He has served on the editorial board of many journals, including *Econometrica*, the *Journal of Economic Literature*, and the *Journal of Economic Perspectives*. In 1998, he was elected fellow of the Econometric Society, and in 2008 he was named Scholar of the College by the College of Liberal Arts, University of Minnesota. His research interests are in banking, in fiscal and monetary policy, and on issues of economic development.

Dr. Devinder Malhotra serves as chancellor of Minnesota State, which includes thirty colleges and seven universities. He previously served in leadership roles at Metropolitan State University and at St. Cloud State University. As chancellor, Malhotra focuses on student success, a commitment to diversity, equity, and inclusion, and programmatic and financial sustainability.

Dr. Bhabani Misra, associate dean at the University of St. Thomas School of Engineering, has been one of the key drivers of the graduate programs in software engineering

Dr. Devinder Malhotra

there for nearly thirty years. Dr. Misra was instrumental in the creation and transformation of innovative programs that have produced more than four thousand master's degree students in the fields of software engineering, data science, information technology, and software management. In the fall of 2017, Dr. Misra earned the prestigious Tekne Lifetime Achievement Award from the Minnesota High Tech Association.

Professor Rama Pandey taught social work at the University of Minnesota in both Duluth and the Twin Cities. A freedom fighter with Mahatma Gandhi during his younger years, he developed courses in international social welfare and peace and social justice.

Dr. Suhas Patankar (mechanical engineering, University of Minnesota) is a pioneer in the field of computational fluid dynamics (CFD) and finite volume method. His book, *Numerical Heat Transfer and Fluid Flow*, is considered a groundbreaking contribution to the CFD field.

Dr. Varanasi Rama Murthy (School of Earth Sciences, University of Minnesota) made several important and innovative contributions to the study of earth and planets. He also served in various administrative roles, including as head of the School of Earth Sciences, associate dean and acting dean in the Institute of Technology (now the College of Science and Engineering), and vice provost and associate vice president for Academic Affairs.

Dr. Suhas Patankar

Dr. Srilata (Sri) Zaheer is dean at the Carlson School of Management, University of Minnesota, where she launched a military veterans initiative to help servicemen and women transition from military to business careers, increased the business community's engagement with the school, and oversaw the introduction of several new programs. Dr. Zaheer holds the Elmer L. Andersen Chair in Global Corporate Social Responsibility, and her research focus is on international business. Her work has

Dr. Sri Zaheer

Niranjana Bashyal and her husband, Ram (originally from Nepal), trained several teachers in Montessori methods in 1972 at a training center and school in St. Paul. Bilquis Dairkee (originally from India) and Freny Irani also were instrumental in promoting Montessori methods in the Twin Cities. *Courtesy Niranjana Bashyal*

Governor Wendell Anderson proclaimed April 1975 Montessori Education Month in Minnesota.
Courtesy Niranjana Bashyal

been honored by the Academy of International Business, by the Academy of Management, including through its PWC Strategy and Eminent Scholar Award, and by the *Minneapolis/St. Paul Business Journal* with its Women in Business Award.

Sonal Desai-Redd (second generation) is the division director of educational programs at Volunteers of America.

Sonal Desai-Redd

In recent years, Indian Americans have contributed in the K-12 education field as teachers and administrators, including *Aroti Bayman* (Minneapolis Public Schools), *Freny Irani* (Seward Montessori School), *Shyamala Jithendranathan* (International Baccalaureate and Gifted and Talented programs director at St. Paul's Central High School), and *Vatsala Menon* (Obama Elementary School).

TV and Newspaper Reporters, Authors, and Communicators

The media is another area in which Indian Americans have brought diversity and are making a mark. Former TV personalities like *Vineeta Sawkar* and journalists such as *Kavita Kumar*, *Neal Justin*, and *Maya Rao* regularly make mainstream contributions. Second-generation Indian American *Geeta Sitaramaiah* (*St. Paul Pioneer Press*) and other journalists have brought attention to the Indian community. *Kashmira Irani* worked as a camera person for KARE. First-generation Indians considered nonnative English speakers and writers like *Vaman Pai* (communications department, City of Minneapolis) and *Kuhu Singh* (online content specialist/contract writer) have made their mark in the communications field. In 2009, *Preeti Mathur* was the first Indian American to be nominated Associate Fellow of the Society for Technical Communication (STC).

Fred de Sam Lazaro is director of the University of St. Thomas's Under-Told Stories Project, which focuses on underreported stories from around the world, including India. He regularly contributes to *PBS NewsHour*, has won several journalism awards, and has served on several boards, including the Asian American Journalists Association.

Fred de Sam Lazaro

Meena Chettiar wrote *Immigration Success: Give Yourself the Best Start in Any Country* and is the founder of Minnesota Shakthi Global Foundation, a nonprofit organization that supports immigrants' career enhancement through education.

Dr. Siva Jasthi, a mechanical engineer, computer scientist, and faculty member at Metropolitan State University, has written seven books for children, including *Let's Play: A Treasury of Traditional Childhood Games from India*.

Jayashree Seth, a 3M chief scientist, has written a book for children: *Namaste! Namaste! . . . And Other Hindi Songs Based on Popular Nursery Rhymes*.

Business and Entrepreneurs

Indian Americans operate an estimated 2,185 businesses in Minnesota, producing about $800 million in sales, an annual payroll of $206 million, and 6,766 jobs.

About 2.9 percent of the Indian American population are entrepreneurs who are responsible for several start-ups such as Kapra Cosmetics, APA Optics (now APA Enterprises), IDeaS, and many others (see below). Among the 3.5 percent who are listed as self-employed, several own businesses such as motels, grocery stores, restaurants, real estate firms, retail enterprises such as dry cleaners or liquor stores, and home-based businesses such as day care, beauty, and alternative medicine services.

Indian entrepreneurs' global business relationships bring investments from around the world; Minnesota is third in the United States for investments by Indian companies. Six Indian companies, mostly in information technology and the telecom industry, are operating in Minnesota today, including Infosys, ITC Infotech, Tata Consultancy Services, and Wipro. Another company, Essar, is involved in the materials and manufacturing sector. A US–India health care summit held in Minneapolis in 2015 brought attention to Minnesota's health care businesses and medical device manufacturing.

Two Indian Americans, Mahendra Nath and Kanta Kuba, have been inducted into the Minnesota Business Hall of Fame.

Suseela Kodali is a software engineer turned entrepreneur who started and later sold her multimillion-dollar business SDK Software and SDK Technical Services. She now consults about small business management, strategic planning, client relationships, process improvement, and product development, among other areas.

Dr. S. K. Dash

Dr. Sita Kantha Dash is an innovator, an entrepreneur, and a prolific and active philanthropist in Minnesota. He is globally recognized for his breakthrough contributions in probiotics, where his pioneering work has been instrumental in the ongoing growth of a $35 billion a year industry.

In 1969, Dr. Dash relocated from Odisha, India, initially landing in South Dakota. He earned his PhD in nutrition and biochemistry from South Dakota State University in 1973 and worked as the director of South Dakota's Food and Drug Commission. He established UAS Laboratories in Minnesota to develop and distribute innovative probiotic products for food, beverages, and nutraceuticals worldwide. He has published more than forty research pieces, is the author of books including *The Consumer Guide to Probiotics,* and cowrote *The Garden Within*.

He serves on twelve boards and has donated funds to more than twenty nonprofit organizations in the Twin Cities, including the Minnesota Historical Society, Hindu Society of Minnesota, Odisha Society of America, and the India Association of Minnesota, and more than ten organizations in India. He established a probiotic and nutraceutical innovation center and an endowed professorship at South Dakota State University. In India, he established the S. K. Dash Center of Excellence of Biosciences and Engineering and Technology (SKBET), which includes funding a chair professor, a visiting scientist, and a postdoctoral fellow at Indian Institute of Technology Bhubaneswar. He has received numerous accolades, honors, and awards for his professional work and for his philanthropy.

In 1988, *Kanta Kuba* founded GCI Systems, based in Shoreview, a company specializing in value-added IT products and services for businesses and nonprofit and governmental organizations. She has been recognized for excellence by the Metropolitan Economic Development Association (MEDA) in Minneapolis and the Minnesota and National Minority Supplier Development Councils. Kuba remembers: "When I started my IT business, I was nearly fifty years old, a female in a male-dominated industry, from India, and without a background in tech or business. I knew how difficult the journey of being an entrepreneur was, especially for women. I had to earn my business every single day. There is no lighted path; you have to create it. You'll constantly be tested, and twists and turns are inevitable. There are many scary moments as a business owner, but you have to believe in yourself first and foremost."

Kanta Kuba

Mahendra Nath came to Minnesota as an engineering student in 1964 but got into business with his wife, Asha, using $5,000 in savings to buy their first property. Nath Companies, founded in 1996, involves the family, including son, daughter, and their spouses. Their hospitality business, comprising restaurants, hotels, and properties, is worth $70 million and employs over a thousand workers. Nath is also a philanthropist who serves on the board of several nonprofits, including the Normandale Community College Foundation Board.

Mahendra Nath

Madhu Reddy came to Minnesota in 1989 to work as a design engineer, eventually becoming vice president of technology at Nortech Systems. In 1994 he founded U.S. Electronics, Inc., which designs LCD displays for multinational companies such as GE Medical (now GE Healthcare), McKesson, Kodak, and more. In 2005, he met President Abdul Kalam to discuss medical imaging technology for low-cost health care in India, which led to a joint venture through the Electronics Corporation of India, Ltd. (ECIL) initiative. He and his wife, Dr. Jyothsna Reddy, are founders of the Sri Venkateswara Temple in Edina.

Mandeep Sodhi is president and chief executive officer at Jobma—Select Source International, which he founded in 1999. Sodhi spent more than a decade working with Delta (Northwest Airlines), Accenture (Andersen Consulting), and Deloitte. His other endeavors include a day-care center, a one-hour photo store, restaurants, nightclubs, and commercial properties.

Mandeep Sodhi

Rajiv Tandon, a serial entrepreneur and an educator, is founder and executive director of the Institute for Innovators and Entrepreneurs at Hamline University and the

author of "Planting Seeds" opinion column in *Twin Cities Business* magazine. His performance enhancement and workforce development company Adayana, Inc., was listed in Inc. 500/5000 fastest-growing companies and the Top 20 Training Outsourcing Companies for five consecutive years. In 2010 *Twin Cities Business* named him one of the "200 Minnesotans You Should Know" for his focus on "EduTech." An advocate for the future of entrepreneurship, he facilitates peer groups of Minnesota CEOs and runs two programs—the Rocket Network and 100 Launches—for propelling ideas into business ventures. He teaches entrepreneurship at the Carlson School of Management at the University of Minnesota.

Rajiv Tandon

Indian Cuisine, Restaurants, and Grocery Stores

Contributing to the food scene and exposing Minnesotans to dishes from all over India—not just the Tandoori North Indian dishes of the past—are several Indian restaurants in Minnesota. There are now more than twenty restaurants in the Twin Cities and one in Rochester as well. Most opened after 2000, when the technology boom brought hundreds of Indians to the state.

In the early years, there were only a few restaurants, mostly serving North Indian–style cuisine. Many did not stay in business for long, but Tandoor, which opened in 1982, is the longest-running Indian restaurant in Minnesota.

Similarly, until the 1990s, only a couple of Indian grocery stores existed in Minnesota. In those early years, many Indians would make frequent trips to Chicago to buy groceries in bulk or order them through the mail. In the late sixties and early seventies, a few Indian grocery items were stocked at stores

Serving the Indian American community in western Minnesota are two Indian and two Nepali/Indian restaurants in the Fargo-Moorhead area: Passage to India, India Palace, Everest Tikka House, and Himalayan Yak. There are no other Indian restaurants in the western half of Minnesota or all of North Dakota.

Khazana Gallery, Minneapolis. *MNHS*

P. C. Mangalick opened India Bazaar in 1970 in Apache Plaza, Minneapolis, which led to other flourishing businesses for the Mangalick family. Here, Magan Agrawal minds the store. *Photo © Mark E. Jensen, courtesy MNHS*

Little India International Market, Minneapolis. *Courtesy author*

NM Designs, Minneapolis. *Courtesy author*

Businesses owned by Indians range from those that cater largely to Indians in Minnesota, such as grocery stores, to others serving the larger community, such as real estate firms, dry cleaners, liquor stores, and motels.

Taj Mahal on Nicollet Mall in Minneapolis was the first Indian restaurant in Minnesota. *MNHS, IAM Archives*

First Time Ever In Twin Cities
SERVING THE NATIVE FOODS OF
INDIA
Indian Cuisine - Vegitarian and Non-Vegitarian
Great American Foods Also.
Open Now—Mon.-Sat. 11 a.m. to 9 p.m.

Taj Mahal
RESTAURANT
1034 Nicollet Mall   Phone 332-9952

Hot Indian Foods, which Amol Dixit started as a food truck, now has four locations, including one at Target Field with a clever tagline: "Hot Twindian. Enough Said." *Courtesy Hot Indian Foods*

In 1997 *Sherbanoo Aziz* moved to be closer to her son, who lived in Comstock, Minnesota, south of Fargo-Moorhead. In 2001, she published a cookbook—*Sherbanoo's Indian Cuisine: Tantalizing Tastes of the Indian Subcontinent*—to introduce her neighbors to Indian cooking. The book led to a series of community education classes and local TV appearances that continue today. After the September 11 attacks, Aziz used her teaching skills to introduce non-Muslims to Islam: community building through shared meals.

like International House of Foods on Washington Avenue in Minneapolis. Later, India House, located in Dinkytown (Minneapolis), sold groceries along with Indian clothes, handicrafts, and jewelry. Today, more than ten Indian grocery stores serve neighborhoods with high concentrations of Indian customers. These include Pooja Grocers and Little India International Market (formerly known as Patel Brothers) on Central Avenue in Minneapolis.

One person who has singularly helped in popularizing Indian food in Minnesota is *Raghavan Iyer*. His first book on Indian cuisine, published under the Betty Crocker banner, put Indian flavors on the table not just for Minnesota cooks but for others as well. Besides *Betty Crocker's Indian Home Cooking*, Iyer has written other cookbooks. He also teaches professional and home cooks, has created TV series, and serves as a restaurant consultant. His Pizza Karma restaurant in Eden Prairie features pizzas with global flavors served on the Indian bread called naan and fired in a tandoor (Indian oven). He also has a mobile phone application, Raghavan's Indian Flavors, featuring recipes and interactive videos.

Raghavan Iyer

8 Looking into the Future

In response to favorable changes in US immigration policy and a demand for professional skills, Indian Americans arrived in Minnesota and set down roots in the Land of Ten Thousand Lakes. Today, with more than forty thousand Indian Americans living and working in the state, the landscape looks vastly different from that of the 1960s and '70s. Indian Americans in Minnesota have become an integral part of the community fabric and are recognized for their many contributions.

Much has changed from those early years when Indian Americans were primarily employed in engineering and medical fields. Today, the shift has been to information technology and computers (33.2 percent in 2017 from 1.6 percent in 1990). Although still primarily employed in STEM areas, many Indian Americans, particularly members of the second generation, have branched into the armed forces, teaching, and social services as well as political and governmental arenas. In 2017, as many as 17.2 percent of Indian Americans were in management positions compared to 7.2 percent in 1990. As an educated immigrant group, with the highest average income and with notable entrepreneurs among their numbers, Indian Americans make major contributions to Minnesota's economy with an estimated buying power of $1.26 billion.

The expanding Indian population and the subsequent growth of Indian grocery stores, restaurants, and opportunities to explore Indian music, dance, and theater have exposed other Minnesotans to India's rich and diverse culture. This has led to more awareness and acceptance of India and of Indians in general—and has also made it easier for newly arrived Indians to assimilate without the hardship faced by those who preceded them.

So, what does the future hold? Current immigration policy changes have already reduced the number of H-1B visas issued for highly skilled labor and are affecting those who are here temporarily; unlike in previous decades, today there are ample opportunities in India and many are choosing to return. However, the United States is still a preferred country for emigration, and Indians are the third-largest country-of-origin group to obtain US lawful permanent residency (LPR) status, after Mexicans and Chinese. As evidenced by the backlog due to quotas set for applying for LPR through employment and family-sponsored means, the trend to stay here permanently is bound to continue.

A look at other parts of the United States shows Indian Americans making great strides in Congress, in Silicon Valley, and in the media. Although the Indian American population in Minnesota is not as large as in New Jersey or California, it is quite probable that Minnesota Indians will continue to contribute at ever-higher levels.

This book represents an initial attempt at capturing and telling the story of Indian Americans in Minnesota through the eyes of the community's members. We hope you have gained an enlightening picture of those who came from India, the Land of the Seven Rivers, and mingled with other immigrants in the Land of Ten Thousand Lakes and the mighty Mississippi.

Acknowledgments

The responsibility of telling the story of Indians in Minnesota for the first time has been a privilege as well as a daunting and challenging experience. I am grateful for many whose help enriched the narratives and made this book possible.

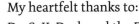

My heartfelt thanks to:

Dr. S. K. Dash and the Dr. Dash Foundation, for the generous grant that spearheaded this book.

The Minnesota Historical Society: Josh Leventhal, for the honor of selecting me to write the book and for overseeing its publication; Erin Cole and Lisa Friedlander, for sharing the research materials from the 2016 *Beyond Bollywood* exhibition; and the Gale Family Library staff, for helping me with research materials, including oral history projects and archived information.

My wonderful editor, Shannon Pennefeather, for not only performing editing magic without changing my voice or style but also for keeping me sane during many frustrating moments. Thanks for always reminding me to keep my eyes on that light at the end of the tunnel and guiding me through this amazing experience.

All of you who shared your stories, memories, and photographs. It was an honor and privilege to record your recollections; without them, the book would have been very dull, indeed.

Ram Gada, Godan Nambudiripad, and Kamala Puram, for reviewing early drafts, for vetting the contents, and for your suggestions. Special thanks to Ram for helping compile the list of contributions by Indians and their success stories.

Sanjukta Chaudhuri, of the Minnesota Department of Employment and Economic Development (DEED), for stepping up at short notice to help me decipher and collect statistics from the census data. Thanks as well to Anjuli Cameron, of the Council on Asian Pacific Minnesotans, and Bruce Corrie, Planning and Economic Development, City of St. Paul, for your help.

Tom LaVenture, for sharing your articles on Indians from the *Asian American Press*, particularly the one on Mohan Sekhon.

My wonderful friends and family members all over the world, thanks for believing in me and for being my constant cheerleaders. Thank you for keeping my spirits up with flowers, dinner invitations, and pep talks.

My husband, Anoop, for your love and support all through what became one of the longest and most challenging projects of my career. Thanks for "encouraging me" to take time off from my regular job, for relieving me of all household tasks, for being my sounding board, my research assistant, and my PR man.

I dedicate this book to my father, Anand Narain Mathur (1925–2008), who lived with us in Minnesota for eighteen years. His parting advice to me when I first left India in 1978 was: "Assimilate and adapt without giving up your values. Do community service; be proud of your culture and share it, but make sure you also learn from others." Daddy, I hope I have made you proud.

Sources Consulted

2012 Survey of Business Owners. "Statistics for All U.S. Firms by Industry, Gender, Ethnicity, and Race for the U.S., States, Metro Areas, Counties, and Places: 2012." Open Data Soft.

Corrie, Bruce P. "Minnesota-India Economic Relations: A Turning Point?" *Minnesota Business*, October 20, 2015.

Historical and Cultural Society of Clay County, with special thanks to programming director Markus Krueger.

Migration Policy Institute, www.migrationpolicy.org:

"Age-Sex Pyramids of Top Immigrant Origin Groups in U.S., 2016."

"Frequently Requested Statistics on Immigrants and Immigration in the United States." March 14, 2019.

"Indian Immigrants in the United States." August 31, 2017.

Maps of Immigrants in the United States: "U.S. Immigrant Population by Metropolitan Area, 2010–2015," and "U.S. Immigrant Population by State and County, 2010–2015."

Minnesota State Demographic Center, Department of Administration. *The Economic Status of Minnesotans 2018*. https://mn.gov/admin/assets/MNSDC_EconStatus _2018Report_FNL_Access.pdf_tcm36-362054.pdf.

Penn Wharton, University of Pennsylvania. Budget Model. "The Effects of Immigration on the United States' Economy." June 27, 2016.

"Percentage of Indians (Asian) in Minnesota by City." Zip Atlas.

Pew Research Center.

US Census Bureau. American FactFinder. "Selected Social Characteristics in the United States, 2011–2015."

US Census Bureau and American Community Survey.

Venkatapuram, Kalpana. "Methods for Ensuring the Continuity of Tradition: A Study of Hindu Community in the Twin Cities." Research paper, 1990.

Wikipedia. "Family Reunification."

Yam, Kimberly. "Asian-Americans Have Highest Poverty Rate in NYC, But Stereotypes Make the Issue Invisible." *Huffington Post*, May 8, 2017.

For Further Reading

Bahadur, Gaiutra. *Coolie Woman: The Odyssey of Indenture*. Chicago: University of Chicago Press, 2013.

Bald, Vivek. *Bengali Harlem and the Lost Histories of South Asian America*. Cambridge, MA: Harvard University Press, 2015.

Bhatia, Sunil. *American Karma: Race, Culture, and Identity in the Indian Diaspora*. New York: New York University Press, 2007.

Indo-American Center Education Committee. *Asian Indians of Chicago*. Images of America. Mount Pleasant, SC: Arcadia Publishing, 2003.

Iyer, Deepa. *We Too Sing America: South Asian, Arab, Muslim, and Sikh Immigrants Shape Our Multiracial Future*. New York: The New Press, 2017.

Jensen, Joan M. *Passage from India: Asian Indian Immigrants in North America*. New Haven, CT: Yale University Press, 1988.

Lal, Vinay. *The Other Indians. A Political and Cultural History of South Asians in America*. Los Angeles: UCLA Asian American Studies Center, 2008.

Lee, Erika. *The Making of Asian America: A History*. New York: Simon & Schuster, 2016.

Prashad, Vijay. *The Karma of Brown Folk*. Minneapolis: University of Minnesota Press, 2001.

Rangaswamy, Padma. *Namasté America: Indian Immigrants in an American Metropolis*. University Park: Pennsylvania State University Press, 2000.

Rudrappa, Sharmila. *Ethnic Routes to Becoming American: Indian Immigrants and the Cultures of Citizenship*. New Brunswick, NJ: Rutgers University Press, 2004.

Index

Page numbers in *italics* indicate illustrations.

Abhinay, 64
Abhisekhar, M. J., 69
Adopt a Senior, 100
adoptees, 26–27
Advani, Dolly, 14, *14, 31*
Advani, Indru, 14, *14*
Advani, Ramona, 14, 85, *104*
aerograms, *37*
Ahuja, Simone, 69
alternative healing, 108, *109*
Ameet, *88, 89*
Anandaraj, Adhithya, 86
Ananya Dance Theatre, 64
Anderson, Wendell, *115*
Anjuman-e-Asghari, 54
Are You Hungry, 100
armed forces, 105–6, *105–6*
Arora, Sant Ram, 18, *18*, 52
Arora, Sudha, 18, *18*
artists, 113
arts organizations, 60–65, *60–65*, 90
Arya, Usharbudh, 49, 108
AshaUSA, 68
Asian American Press, 38
Asian Indian American Republicans of
    Minnesota, 102
Asian Indian Women's Association (AIWA),
    60, *68*
Asian Indians, 4
Asiatic Barred Zone Act (1917), 5
assimilation, 30–32, *31–34*
Athletes Committed to Educating Students
    (ACES), 100
Autobiography of a Yogi (Yogananda), 11–12
Aziz, Sherbanoo, 120

Babu, Neelima, 67
baby showers, 45
Bains, Sarjit, 68–69, *69*
Baisakhee, 42
Baldwin, Ella, 38
Balroop, Satya, 53
BAPS Shri Swaminarayan Mandir, 53, *53*
Barrett, Trevor, 61
Bashyal, Niranjana, *114*
Bashyal, Ram, *114*
Bayman, Aroti, *115*
Belani, Kumar G., 111, *111*
Beyond Bollywood exhibit, 98, *99*
Bharat School, 67. *See also* School of India for
    Languages and Culture (SILC)
Bharat Sevashram Sangha, 53
Bharati, Swami Veda, 108
Bhatnagar, Anil, 58
Bhatt, Harshad (Hap), *79*, 79–80
Bhatt, Paurvi, 110–11, *111*
Bhatt, Rekha, 80
Bollywood films, 70
brain drain, 20
Buddhism, 56
Bullinga, Roswitha, *46*
business: leaders, 110–11, *111*, 116–20, *117–20*, 121;
    sales, payrolls, and employees, 8

Cameron, Anjuli Mishra, 80
Camp Masala, 26
CAPI USA (formerly Centre for Asian and
    Pacific Islanders), 100
ChaiCity, 69
Chari, V. V., 113
charity and charitable organizations, 74, *74–75*,
    98, 100–101, *100–101*
Chatterjea, Ananya, 64

Chaudhary, Raj, 68, 69
Chaudhary, Ravi, 102–3, *103*, 106
Chaudhary, Satveer, 103–4, *104*
Cherucheril, Kurian, 17
Chettiar, Meena, 116
children of immigrants, 85–86, 96, 97
Chinmaya Mission, 53
Chrastek, Jody, *27*, 28
Christianity, 54
citizenship status, 8, *31*, 102
clothing, *46*, 84, *91*
communications, 38–39, 115–16, *116*
Compassionate Action for Animals, 100
Connect India, *59*
Continental Cricket Club, 70, 72
Corelle Ware dishes, 39
Corrie, Bruce, *104*, 105
countries of origin, 5, 6
culture: arts organizations, 60–65, *60–65*,
    90; sharing and showcasing, 23, 43, 58, 91,
    91–97, 94, 96–98; women as preservationists
    of, 84

Dairkee, Bilquis, *114*
dance organizations, 63–64, *63–64*, 72, 90
darshan, 50
Dasari, Bhushan Rao, 54
Dash, Kalpana, *101*
Dash, Sita Kantha, 75, 101, 117, *117*
death, 80–81
demographics, 5–9, 22, 23
Desai, Bhupat, 14, *14–15*
Desai, Jagadish, 17, 46, 58, 73
Desai, Kumud (Sumita), *14*, 15
Desai, Parag, 106, *106*
Desai, Ravi, 47
Desai, Roswitha Bullinga, 46
Desai-Redd, Sonal, 115, *115*
discrimination, examples of, 77–78
divorce, 85
Diwali (festival of lights), 40, *41*, 52
Dixit, Amol, 119
Dixit, Nayana, 3, *3*, 22
Dixit, Padmakar K., *16*; as early settler, 16,
    22; with family (1962), *3*; as Hindu priest,
    46, *46*, 80; home in Minneapolis, *30*;
    IMSOM and, 61; position at University
    of Minnesota, 3
Dixit, Shreya, *81*, 82
Dixit, Vijay, 82
Dixit, Vimala, *3*, 16
domestic abuse, 80, 84–85
Dr. Dash Foundation, 100
Dr. V. Premanand Theatre and Concert Hall

and scholarships at Normandale Commu-
    nity College, Bloomington, 101
Dreamland Arts, 65
Dussehra, *41*, 43
Dutt, Raj, 58
Dutta, Milin, 89, *89*, 100

East African Indians, 25–26
Eden Prairie, 29
education: cost of, 19–20; honors, 86, *86*;
    leaders in, 5, 113–15, *113–15*; levels achieved,
    5, 6, 7; organizations supporting, 100;
    paperwork needed, 23; School of India for
    Languages and Culture (SILC), 26, 63, 66,
    67, 97; schools, 67
Education Foundation, 100
employment: companies hiring and sponsor-
    ing, 5, 20–21, 23; occupations, 5, 6, 7, 23, 121;
    of women, 84
entertainment: movies, 70, 73; radio, 68–69, *69*;
    sports, 70, *71*, 72; television, 69, *69*. *See also*
    specific organizations
entrepreneurs. *See* business

family life: aerograms, 37; festivals and, 39–40,
    42–43, *43*; importance of, 8–9; life events
    celebrations, 45–47, *45–49*; multigenera-
    tional homes, 9, *36*, 86–87; religion at home,
    50, *50*; reunification after 1965 law, 19, 87;
    telephone calls, 36–37; visits, 35–36
Festival of Nations, 91, *91–93*
festivals: American, 43, 44, 45; Jains and, 56;
    overview of, 39–40, 41–43, *43*; women's, 43;
    Zoroastrian, 56. *See also specific celebrations*
55+ Senior Group, 16, 60, 87, *87*
food, *31*, 39, 118, *119–20*, *120*
Fossen, Rolf, 14
Franklin, Gummadi, 20
Franklin, Shirley, 20

Gada, Neena, 18, *18*, 20, 49, 67, 73
Gada, Ram, 20, 73; as early settler, 18, *18*, 20;
    Jain Center and, 55; marriage, 49; oral histo-
    ry projects, 96; public service by, 105
Gaddam, Babu N., 109, *109*
Ganesh Chaturthi, 43
Ganguli, Aparna, 83
Geeta Ashram, 52, *52*, 53
Geetmala, 69, *69*
Golu, 43
government, 102–5, *102–5*
Grainger, Margaret, 22
green cards, 20–21
Gujarati Samaj, *41*, 43

Gulati, Suraksha, 69
Gupta, Madhuka, 58
Gupta, Shashi, 68–69, 69
Gurdwara, 55
Guyana, 24

H-1B visas: created, 5, 23; nickname for people
    with, 32
Haldi Kumkum, 43
Hati House, 17
Henderson, Margaret Doris, 13, 13
Hindu Mandir, 41, 51–52
Hindu Samaj Temple and Cultural Center,
    53
Hindu Society of Minnesota, 51, 98
Hinduism: beliefs, 50; official recognition
    by Minnesota of, as religion, 46; organi-
    zations, 51, 53; religious speakers for, 53;
    temples, 51–52, 51–53; vandalism of Maple
    Grove temple, 78
Hirekerur, Sandeep, 72
Hlavka, Sara, 49
Holi, 41
holidays, 39–40, 42–43, 43
homes, 9, 36, 86–87
Hooroo, Sam, 81
Hopkins, 30
Hot Indian Foods, 119
Hoyle, Robert, 58
Humphrey, Hubert, 26
Hussain, Abid, 73

I-94 form, 23
immigrants: British policy and, 14; characteris-
    tics of, 4; lawful permanent residency (LPR)
    status, 121–22; laws regulating, 2, 3, 5, 19, 23,
    87; second wave (1965–90), 19–22, 83; third
    wave (1990s–2000s), 23
immigrants, first wave (pre-1965): domestic
    chores, 21; green cards during, 21; items
    brought by, 21, 21; obtaining employment,
    20–21; oral history project interviews, 96,
    96; settlers, 3, 3, 16–19, 16–19; students,
    12–15, 12–15; visitors, 11, 11–12
Immigration Act (1917), 5
Immigration Act (1990), 5, 23
Immigration and Nationality Act (1945), 2, 3
Immigration and Nationality Act (1965), 5, 19,
    87
income levels, 7, 29
India: Independence Day festival, 43, 44;
    officially recognized languages and dialects
    in, 57; visits to and from family in, 35–36;
    weddings in, 46

India Abroad, 38
India Association of Minnesota (IAM,
    formerly India Club), 103; Connect India
    (originally IAM Dinner), 59; IndiaFest,
    23, 43, 58, 94, 94–95; oral history projects,
    96–97, 96–98; original name, 21; overview
    of, 58, 60
India Club. See India Association of Minnesota
    (IAM, formerly India Club)
India House, 120
India Tribune, 38
IndiaFest, 23, 43, 58, 94, 94–95
Indian American Muslim Council, 54
Indian diaspora: adopted children, 26–27;
    defining, 23–24; East African, 25–26;
    Indo-Caribbean and Malaysian, 24–25;
    missionaries' children, 27–28, 27–28
Indian Music Society of Minnesota (IMSOM),
    60–61, 60–61
Indian Students Association (ISA, at Univer-
    sity of Minnesota, formerly Indo-American
    Club), 57, 57–58, 58
Indo-American Association of the Great Plains
    (IAAGP), 60
Indo-American Club Newsletter, 70
Indo-Caribbean Indians, 24–25
InFusion, 61
inventions, 109, 109–10
Irani, Freny, 114, 115
Irani, Kashmira, 115
Islam, 54
Islamic Center, 54
Iyer, Raghavan, 88, 88–89, 120, 120

Jacob, Pennamma, 17, 17
Jain, Sangeeta, 104
Jainism, 55–56
Jaiswal-Dale, Ameeta, 113
Jasthi, Siva, 116
Jithendranathan, Shyamala, 115
John, K. K., 54
Johnson, Lyndon, 5, 19
Johnston, Kurt, 24
Jones, Samuel, 54
Judaism, 56
Junghare, Indira, 113
Justin, Neal, 115

Kalam, Abdul, 73
Kamath, Ashwin, 107
Kamath, Ullas, 52
Kamran, Kunal, 52
Kamran, Sujan, 107
Karva Chauth, 43

Kashkari, Neel, *104*, 105
Katha Dance Theatre, 63, *63*, 98
Kaul, T. N., *73*
Kenya, 25
Keshaviah, V., 61
Khanna, Gopal, *104*, *104*
Kharbanda, Basant, 15, *15*
Kharbanda, Veena, 15, *15*
Kiffmeyer, Mary, *103*
Klobuchar, Amy, *102*
Kocherlakota, Narayana Rao, 105
Kodali, Suseela, 116
Kokatnur, V., *12*
Komanduri, Sesha, 46, 49
Krishan, Ram, 61
Krishnan, Vaidyanathan, 81
Kshettry, Vibhu, 111, *111*
Kuba, Kanta, 116, 117, *117*
Kumar, K. S. P., *17*, 17–18, 21
Kumar, Kavita, 115
Kumar, Renu, 64
Kumar, Sanjai, 106
Kumar, Usha, 17–18, 67

languages: officially recognized, and dialects
    in India, 57; School of India for Languages
    and Culture, 26, 63, *66*, *67*, 97; use of
    American slang, 32
LaVenture, Tom, 38
Lazaro, Fred de Sam, 116, *116*
LGBTQ+ community, 88–89, *88–89*
Little India International Market (formerly
    known as Patel Brothers), *119*, 120
Luce-Celler Act (1946), 5

Madia, J. Ashwin, *106*, *106*
magazines, 38–39
Mahapatra, Sarat, *58*
Maharaj, Birju, *72*
Maharaj, Swami Harihar, 52
Mahmood, Talat, 74
Maiya, Divya, 64, *64*
Malaysian Indians, 24–25
Malhotra, Devinder, 113, *113*
Mangalick, P. C., 51, *119*
Mangalick, Rashi, 64
Mangalick, Shanti, 51
Mangalick, Shashi, *48*, 49
Mangalick family home, 30
marriage: arranged, 45, *49*; divorce, 85; inter-
    racial and interreligious, 31, 45, 46, 46–47,
    47; interracial and interreligious, and
    children, 85–86; rate, 9; weddings, 45, 46,
    49, *91*
Mathur, Anoop, *20*

Mathur, Manila, 69
Mathur, Pramod, 64, 69
Mathur, Preeti, 67, 116
Mathur, Shruti, *47*, 86
Mathur, Sujan, 107
McLaren, Deborah, 27
media, 38–39, 68–69, *69*, 115–16, *116*
medicine, 13, *13–14*, 108, 111–13, *111–13*
Meditation Center, 108
Menon, Raj, 30, 96
Menon, Vatsala, 96, 115
Mestenhauser, Joseph, 22
Minneapolis Daily Star, 12
Minneapolis Journal, 13
Minneapolis Meditation Group
    of Self-Realization Fellowship,
    108
Minnesota Asian Indian Democratic
    Association, 102, *102*
Minnesota Asian Indian Directory, 58
Minnesota Hindu Dharmic Sabha Vishnu
    Mandir, 52
Minnesota Hindu Milan Mandir, 53
Minnesota Indian Cricket Team, 71
Misra, Bhabani, 113–14
Misra, Induprava, 16, *16–17*
Misra, Niru, 16, *16–17*, 22
Misra, Sudhanshu, 16, *16–17*, 30
Mistry, Zaraawar, 65, *65*
Mitra, Sumita, 110, *110*
Mody, Kokila, 19, *19*, 70
Mody, Sy, 18–19, *19*, 58
movement, 70
movies, 70, 73
Mukherjee, Dipankar, 64, *64*
Munda, Ram Dayal, 74
Murthy, Kamakshi Murthy, 31, *31*
Murthy, Varanasi Rama, 19, 114
Murthy, Venkata Krishna, 31
music organizations, 60–62, *60–62*
Muslim organizations, 54
Mustaphi, Rita, 63, 67
Muthyala, Ramaiah, 111–12

Nadathur, Prerna, 86
Naik, Arvind, 108
Nair, Prabha, 67
Naithani, Alli, *47*
Naithani, Jayesh, *47*
Nambudiripad, Godan, 96
Nambudiripad, Unny, 100
Nanak (Sikh Guru), 54
Narayan, Dharani, *73*
Narayanan, P. G., 105, *105*
Natarajan, Meena, 64, *64*

Nath, Asha, 15, *15*, 117
Nath, Deepak, *49*
Nath, Mahendra, 15, *15*, 100, 116, 117, *117*
Nath Foundation, 100
National Origins Act (1924), 5
Navratri (celebrations before Dussehra), *41*, 43
Nayak, K. Suresh, 58
newspapers, 38–39
Nigam, Ram, *81*
Nityanadan, Nirupama (Rani), *90*
NM Designs, *119*
non-resident Indians (NRIs), 24
Noronha, June, 25–26
Norton, Lisa, *36*
Norton, Thomas, *36*
NRI Homecoming, 74

occupations, 5, 6, 7, 23, 121
Onam (harvest festival), 42
oral history projects, 96–97, *96–98*
organizations, 57–58, *59*, 60–65, 67–68. *See also specific organizations*
Orr, Leslye, 65
Out In the Backyard—Cultural Wellness Center, 100
Overseas Citizenship of India (OCI), 36

Pai, Mohan, 107
Pai, Naveen, 107
Pai, Vaman, 115
Pai, Vinay, 107
Pandey, Rama, 114
Pangea World Theater, 64, *65*
Parents of Indian Children (PIC, later Programs for Indian Children), 26
Parsism, 56
Pasricha, Anupama, 113
Patankar, Suhas, 114, *114*
Patel, Anjana, *46*
Patel, Gunvant, *48, 49*
Patel, Indra, 38, *46*
Patel, Kalyanji, 19
Patel, Punjabhai, *108*
Patel, Ria, *81*, 82
Patel, Vimla, 19
Pathre, Minakshi (Minu), 79, *79*
Pathre, Rijutha, 67, *79, 79*
Pathre, Sadanand, *79, 79*
Paulose, Rachel, *104, 104–5*
Pavan, A., 62
Pavan, Pooja Goswami, 62, *62*
Peterson, Myrna, *22*
Peterson, Stephen, *34*
Pizza Karma, 120

politics and government, 102–5, *102–5*
Pongal (harvest festival), 42
Pooja Grocers, 120
population, 5, 22, 23
Prakash, Ekta, 100
Premanand, Jayaseetha, 78, 101
Premanand, Visvanatha, 58, 61, 101
Programs for Indian Children, 26
public libraries, 38
public service, 102–5, *102–5*
puja altars, *50*
Puram, Askhita, *45*
Puram, Kamala, *45*, 68
Puri, Aarti, 106
Puri, Om, 70
Puri, Varun, 106

radio programs, 68–69, *69*
Radio Sangam, 68–69, *69*
Ragamala Dance Company, 63, 72, 97
Rajan, Raj V., 110, *110*
Rajasekar, Nirmala, 62, *62*, 94
Rajender, Shyamala, 77–78
Rakhee (or Raksha) Bandhan, 41
Ramakrishnan, Nayana, 20, 22
Ramakrishnan, Ram, 20
Ramakrishnan, Seshaaiyar, 75
Ramamoorthy, Senthilkumar, *100*
Ramanathan, Anu, *46*
Ramanathan, Sekhar, *46*
Ramanathan, Vijay, 61
Ramaswamy, Aparna, 72
Ramaswamy, Ranee, 63, *63, 72*
Rambachan, Anantanand, 24–25, *25*
Rambachan, Ishanaa, 86
Ramer, Anil, 27, *27*
Ramer, Bob, 27, 28
Ramer, Nancy, 27, 28
Ramer, Rob, 27, *27*, 28
"Ramsgate" (Hopkins), 30
Rao, Maya, 115
Rao, Vikram, *48, 49*
Rathayatra (chariot festival), 41
Reddy, Jyothsna, *101*, 118
Reddy, Madhu, *101*, 118
Reddy Foundation, 101
Rein, Dan, 96
religion: Buddhism, 56; Christianity, 54; Indo-Caribbean Indians and, 24; Islam, 54; Jainism, 55–56; Judaism, 56; Sikhism, 54–55, *55*; statistics, 50; Zoroastrianism (Parsism), 56. *See also* Hinduism
R. G. K. Modern Indian Dance Company, 64
Ria Patel Foundation, 101
Rjender, Shyamala, 58

Roberts, Leah, 26
Rochester, 30

Sandgren, Peter, *48*, 49
Sane, Kumud, 51, 112, *112*
Sane, Shashikant, 46, 51, 112, *112*
Sarkar, Shantanu, 110, *110*
Satyarthi, Kailash, *73*
Satyarthi, Sumedha, *73*
Sawkar, Vineeta, 115
Saxena, Krishna, 51, 100, 112, *112*
Saxena, Kusum, 51, 100, 112, *112*
Scholberg, Dolores, *28*
Scholberg, Henry, 28, *28*
School of India for Languages and Culture (SILC): adopted Indian children and, 26; dance companies and, 63; oral history project interviews, 97; overview of, *66, 67*
Sekhon, Mohan Singh: as early settler, 13, *13*–14; family, 13; home, 30; in US Army, *105*
Sekhon, Sylvia, 13, *13*–14
Self-Realization Fellowship, 12
senior citizens, 86–88, *87*, 100
Seth, Jayshree, 110, *110*, 116
Sethna, Patarasp Rustomji, 16, *16*
settlement patterns, 29–30, 31, 39
SEWA–Asian Indian Family Wellness (SEWA–AIFW): about, 68; domestic abuse programs, 80, 84–85; services for senior citizens, *87*, 87–88
Shah, Kusum, 55
Shah, Rajiv, 100, 112, *112*
Shah, Ramnik, 25
Shah, Shanti, 34, 67
Shah, Vinod, 55
Shah, Vishant, 47
Shankar, Ananth, *102*
Sharma, Asha, 80
Sheeso, Darlene, 22
Shikha, Deep, 113
Shortridge, Emily, *47*
Shree Satyam Mandir, 52–53
Shreya R. Dixit Memorial Foundation, 101
Shri Gaayatri Mandir, 53
Shukla, Har, 31
Sikhism, 54–55, *55*
Sikka, Daljit, 55
Singapore, 24
Singaram, Nicole, 78–79
Singaram, Shanthi, 78–79
Singh, Ann Marie, 24
Singh, Bash, 58, 79

Singh, Harry, 24
Singh, Hira, 12–13
Singh, Kehar, 55
Singh, Paul, 79
Singh, Ramraj, 24
Singh, Sant Rajinder, 108
Sister Edith, *17*
Sitaramaiah, Geeta, 115
small-town life, 31, *31*
social service organizations, 67–68, 80
Sodhi, Mandeep, 118, *118*
Somasundaram, Jaya, 78
Somasundaram, Rathna, 78
Sonnifer, Polly, 96
Sood, Amit, 112, *112*
Sounds of India, 69, *69*
South Asian Arts and Theater House (SAATH), 64
Sri Saibaba Mandir, 53
Sri Venkateswara (Balaji) Hindu Temple, 53
Subrahmanian, Krishnan, 112–13, *113*
Sukatme, Vasant, *58*
Sury, Priya M., 86

Tadavarthy, Geeta, *48*, 49
Taj Mahal (restaurant), *119*
Tandon, Rajiv, 118, *118*
Tandon, Veeti, *48*, 49
Tandoor (restaurant), 118
Tanzania, 25
television programs, 69, *69*
terminology, 4
Thakur, Mukhtar, 68–69
Tharoor, Lily, 24
theater organizations, 64–65, *65*, 90
Tirtha, Swami Rama, 12, 13
Trinidad and Tobago, 24
Truman, Harry, 5
Twin Cities and suburbs, 29–30

Uganda, 25
University of Minnesota: first wave faculty, 16, *16*, 17, *17*–18, 19; first wave students, 12, *12*–13, 14; host families, 22, *22*; Indian Students Association, 57, *57*–58, *58*; International Students Office, 22, *22*

Vaisakhi, 42
Vakil, Jinal, 64
Valli, Alarmél, *72*
Varadachari, V. C., 58
Varalakshmi, 43
visas: H-1B visas, 5, 23, 32; Overseas Citizenship of India and, 36; paperwork for, 23

Vivekananda, Swami, *12*
Vora, Geeta, *84*, 101
Vora S.E.R.V.I.C.E., 101

weddings, 45, *46, 46*, 91
wellness organizations, 67–68
Wellstone, Paul, 27, *103*
women: arrival in second wave of, 83; Asian Indian Women's Association (AIWA), 60, 68; bridal attire, *46*, 91; discrimination against, 77–78; domestic abuse and, 84–85; employment of, 84; as primary caregivers and preservationists of Indian culture, 84; traditions and festivals for, *41, 43. See also specific individuals*

yoga classes, 10, *10*, 108–9
Yogananda, Swami Paramahansa, *10*, 11–12

Zaheer, Srilata (Sri), *114, 114–15*
Zdenek, F. F., 58
Zoroastrianism, 56

British airways ब्रिटिश ऐअरवेज

Preeti Mathur, with her father (left, front) and in-laws, departs Mumbai (then called Bombay) for Minnesota on April 15, 1978.

About the Author

Preeti Mathur, an instructional designer and technical communication consultant, is a longtime Twin Cities resident and an active member of the Indian American community in Minnesota. She is a founding member of the School of India for Languages and Culture (SILC) and a past board member of the India Association of Minnesota (IAM) and the Minnesota Literacy Council (MLC).